may be

D1345656

What Shall I Wear?

The What, Where, When and How Much of Fashion

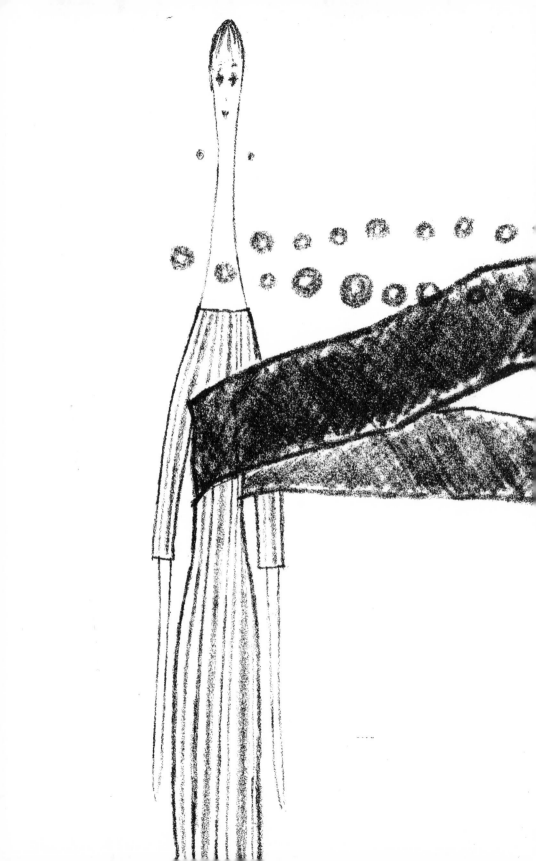

What Shall I Wear?

The What, Where, When and How Much of Fashion

Claire McCardell

Illustrations by Annabrita

OVERLOOK/ROOKERY
NEW YORK, NEW YORK

WHAT SHALL I WEAR?

This edition first published in The United States of America in 2012 by
The Rookery Press, Tracy Carns Ltd.
in association with The Overlook Press
141 Wooster Street
New York, NY 10012
www.therookerypress.com
www.overlookpress.com

For information about bulk and special sales contact sales@overlookny.com

WHAT SHALL I WEAR?
The What, Where, When and How Much of Fashion by Claire McCardell
First published in 1956 by Simon & Schuster
This edition typography, design and layout copyright ° 2012 The Rookery Press

Library of Congress Catalog Card Number: 56-11190

Printed in the United States of America

ISBN 9781-58567-970-6

10 9 8 7 6 5 4 3 2 1

CONTENTS

CHAPTER 1

WHAT IS FASHION?

W**HAT IS FASHION?** What do I really know about it? And who am I to tell about it?

I who love some twenty-year-old dresses far better than the latest look. I who must nevertheless have new clothes, and want them, and look forward to everything that does with them. The excitement of a new line . . . the feel of the right color . . . the eternal chances I know I'm going to take with material and texture and places and people—all mixed up with clothes. And the fun of it all.

Fashion should be fun, and whenever I am tempted to take it too seriously, if I design something that asks for a pedestal in the Museum of Modern Art, I am tumbled down to earth by the blunt voice of a buyer: "Where would you wear it?" And mentally I applaud because I believe that clothes are for real, live women, not for pedestals. They are made to be worn, to be lived in. Not to walk around on models with perfect figures.

But to go on trying to find out what fashion is:

Fashion is elusive.

Some people have it without knowing it—some people know it without having it. Consider the peasant girl who knows how to tie her kerchief. Consider the art student who doesn't—even though she's majoring in Fashion Design.

What you do with Fashion makes it Fashion. The right proportion, this much red, this much white, this much blue; it makes flags and it makes well-dressed women. The right

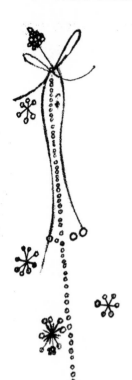

combination counts. And you can't look it up in the dictionary. The right shoes, the right hat, the right bag, the extra color, the necklace or scarf—or the thing that made you think of it all. There are no permanent rules. A fashion that is here today may be gone tomorrow—and back the next day. But I can promise you that if you use your eyes, train your eyes, you will soon learn to recognize the woman with a sense of Fashion.

Fashion is contradictory.

I hate anything that looks too new in a brassy sense—but I can't imagine not trying new color combinations, new ways to tie a sash, new hats, new angles . . . even new postures. Moving my waistline around—up, down—or deciding to have none at all.

Fashion makes rules.

Hems—by day, by night, when short, when long, in what year? And does eight inches or twelve from the floor look the same on all women no matter what shape they are, what heel-height they're wearing? Of course not. So . . .

Fashion breaks rules.

Be flexible, it warns you. Keep a stern eye on yourself. Where do jackets end in the Fashion magazines? Where *should* they end on *you*? Waist-length, hip-length, finger-tip, tunic? Obviously something besides Fashion reportage enters into your choice of clothes. The Fashion magazines might not have mentioned the bolero—but this short little miracle that avoids the waistline is a wonderful way to disguise the less-than-perfect dimension.

Fashion is a calendar, a clock, a date-book, a quiz program.

Short gloves, eight-button, twelve-button—and don't forget the really long white ones for a ball. Fashion tells you which to buy for when, for where. What goes with what? But *why*? And who says so? The last question is important. People without a sense of fun, of dash, of whim, may misunderstand Fashion. If your maiden aunt finds a ladybug on the lapel of your suit unamusing, don't blame the maiden aunt. Blame yourself. You have worn the ladybug for the wrong audience. And how stern is your eye on *yourself*? Are you tea-dancing in the supermarket? Are you a secretary dressing like a siren? Is your mink a rat? Is your Hunting Pink really Shocking? Is your age *really* a secret? And are you by any chance trying to dress for a fashion-magazine audience instead of your husband? Beware if he says: "Well, who are you trying to impress tonight?" Stunning is all right—but who wants to be stunning if it's going to stun—not only your husband but everyone who knows you?

Fashion is change.

Fashion puts in shoulder pads—then takes them away. I never had so much fun as the year I ripped them all out. Unless it was the year when Fashion said that big head-fitting hats were coming back. I couldn't wait until they appeared in the stores. I hiked down to milliner's row for an unblocked felt, poked it high, pulled it low, and an interesting thing happened. The one new hat shape made me take stock of other hats lying around. Unless you are 100 per cent puritan about stripping your closets of yesterday's clothes, you've probably got some hats that date way back. Some of the oldest will suddenly look up-to-date. The excitement of one new idea often brings your whole wardrobe into line.

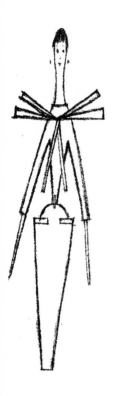

Fashion is an influence.

You may set a trend, you may be a mouse, you may invest in smart clothes because of your job, or give up smart clothes because of your husband. But one thing you can be sure of: what you wear is going to influence your life and what others think about you. Some people have the touch—they can absorb new ideas and make them their own. Others are lost and afraid. They don't even realize a change until it is two years old. Sometimes it is better to be a mouse, to fade into your own background. And you won't really envy the woman who dresses for instant recognition value because you like your own background best. There is a great deal to be said for the woman who *knows* what she should wear. Some jobs, some temperaments, some husbands, like the latest thing in Fashion. I think of myself as a continuous experiment, a testing ground for ideas. That's why you'll find a black peasant-cape in my wardrobe, picked up in the store in Paris where the peasants go to buy their capes. Naturally I don't wear it in the fields. I wear it over my ski clothes, to football games— and sometimes on a rainy night to the theatre.

And now, perhaps, we come to the question of who am I to write about Fashion? First of all, I am a woman. Quite secondarily, I am a designer. Sometimes I am a hostess. Sometimes I am a guest. I have a job to go to. I have a market list to plan. I *love* clothes. I have loved them since the days when I cut paper dolls from the Fashion magazines, and I think the way the scissors followed the lines of Fashion had a great deal to do with my Fashion education.

I have seen Fashion as business. Sizes—colors—buyers —models—salesmen—saleswomen—swatches—piece goods—stores—fashion magazines. I have also seen Fashion in action—how it looks when you move—walking, travelling, flying, hitting a golf ball, skiing and sailing. I have seen Fashion in tune with background—place, climate, occasion. And I have asked myself the thousands of questions that anything to do with Fashion will always pose.

What shall I wear? Where would I wear *that*? What is my size—and does it fit? Where is my waistline today? What color with what? Am I the type? Is anyone?

Fashion lets you choose.

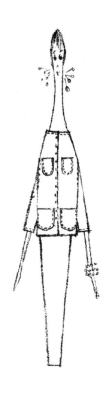

Don't try to live up to Fashion. First of all, stay firmly you. And if Fashion seems to be saying something that isn't right for you, ignore it. Make your own mixtures—in jewelry as in jackets. Don't try to be a type. Too often you have heard the word *type* and have tried to wriggle yourself into the definition. Pretty type. Smart type. Casual type. Arty type. Each implies overemphasis. And if you academically try to choose which is you, you are going to find yourself in trouble.

When pretty is too pretty, your audience is going to be conscious of flutter and lace and everything trailing, including probably your overcurled hair. Too smart may be as coldly impersonal as a decorator's showroom where even the matchbox must stay in place. Overemphasis can be disastrous and true Fashion wouldn't want it that way—and the truly fashionable woman couldn't be that way. Everything in Fashion is *how much, how little*, not *too much, too little*—whether color or jewelry or fur or crinolines or the brim of your hat.

Everything in Fashion is also *when* and *where*, which will bear repeating in every chapter in this book. "I hate crinolines," I said passionately one day. Then I stopped to think. "I don't really hate crinolines. I just hate them in a crowded elevator in the middle of a busy day. And I hate them when they look uneven and sloppy—holding out a horrible fabric never meant to go over so much stiffness." If you try to make the current fashion work everywhere, it will defeat you. And instead of fun, it will be a worry and an embarrassment.

Do you fall in love with a dress just because it is shown in a glossy fashion magazine? Don't forget that a fashion magazine is more or less a dream book. Take a good look at the

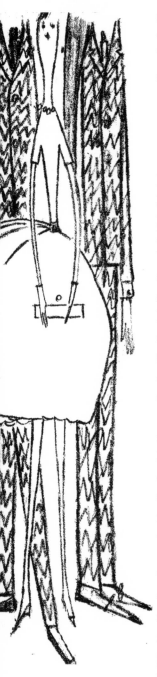

model who is wearing the dress. Can your figure compete with hers? Are you as impeccably groomed? Will your husband worry about the neckline? Where is she wearing it? In a fashion magazine! Where would you wear it?

Fashion should be explored.

And now, having warned you to be cautious, I shall urge you to be brave. Look at new fashions and see if they can be yours. Test the way they fit, feel, look—how they are supposed to be worn—how you will wear them. You'll find you have enormous choice. Gingham and calico vs. satin and mink. Usually not to be mated otherwise—although jersey and flannel have been known to invite a satin touch, and silk often asks for a wool jersey sash. Temperament plays a part here. I happen to like black jersey and caviar. You may like black satin and caviar. Wear the fabric you feel best in. That's a number-one rule. (A small word of caution though. While caviar is both a lunchtime and cocktail hour delicacy, black satin is too dressed up for lunch.)

Explore Fashion and say No if you are temperamentally incapable of starting a trend. Wait for the first wave of big hats if you are afraid you might duck. But if you do decide to date the "wild hat"—remember to hold your head high in spite of the whistles and giggles that may greet it. Later your friends will probably say, "You know, you were the first to wear it, and now everybody's got one."

You can also wait too long to buy a new idea—it may be "old hat" by the time you discover it, which can result in a very bad investment. Part of the fun of Fashion is the excitement of change. And Fashion isn't meant to be taken too seriously. Sometimes it is a whim, frivolous and silly on purpose. But if you are afraid of looking silly or feeling silly in the hat with the butterflies perched on the crown, the hat is not for you. Not even if it wears the label of a famous designer and costs enough to prove that Fashion is big business.

Even the Fashion magazines (whose whole reason for

being depends on Fashion) are willing to wink at it. How often they show you its gay side, write about it with humor, pose it amusingly. A model vamps you with a fantastic umbrella or a provocatively placed mole. She is quite openly kidding Fashion. And Fashion can take it—even thrives on it.

Fashion says Don't wait.

But a wise word is, *do*—for at least a second thought. You should always analyze a drastic change before you buy it. If you can afford to give a dress away after one wearing, be as happy-go-lucky as you please. But it is important to realize that a radical change in fashion is often accompanied by question marks. It may be a wonderfully right idea, executed wrongly—or not exactly right in the beginning. The wrongs are righted in time and the fashion becomes established. But the woman who accepted the fashion the first day it was advertised may be sorry she didn't wait for a while.

The ballet slipper that grew a little heel and brought low heels into our lives is a good example. It was a direct result of the war. As a ballet slipper, it could be bought without a shoe coupon. It was fine for the living room, the country club, cocktails on the terrace. Not so fine for the subway. It slipped and slopped along New York streets. It probably hurt a good many feet that needed support. But it was a *right* fashion. It taught women who had been wearing nothing but high heels for years that no heel or very little heel could be attractive and that the shell shape was flattering. Today, the ballet slipper has been refined into a little shoe that has kept the charm of simple closed-toe ballet design, but it has been submitted to craftsmen who have made it adaptable for street wear.

But don't get in a shoe rut. You are not going to go permanently into no heels or low heels just because you have discovered them. Remember how Fashion sense is largely made up of time sense and place sense. With certain clothes, heels are important—the higher the better. And conversely, with

certain clothes, any heel is out of the question. Yet I *have* seen long wool socks mismatched with wedgies, and a wedge heel that looms so high it might as well belong to stilts.

One toenail peeking from an almost closed pump seems to me one of the great horrors of the shoe business—yet many people call such shoes comfortable. Soft shoe construction can ease the pain of hard shoes and can cover toes in comfort. When you wear sandals, let *all* your toes show; nature has provided lines that are flattering to the body—stick to them. There are certain clothes that we wear today that really look best with bare feet. The thong sandal is the closest approximation to the barefoot look. Thong sandals with a little heel seem to be exactly right with one of my long loose-flowing summer evening dresses.

If you like to talk, don't forget the joy of low or medium heels. If you like to walk in the woods, remember comfortable light boots—don't collect all the burrs in the countryside. And be sure your toes can wiggle in your boots. Feeling numb is almost as bad as being frostbitten.

Climate, scenery, even national customs can affect what you wear. I shall never forget the high hat with plumes that I fell in love with in Paris. A London cockney laughed out loud when he saw me wearing it next to a plumed guard at Buckingham Palace. Only the King wore it there.

And what you are doing when you are in your clothes counts too. Don't try to wear the dress that you are literally poured into when you board an airplane. You'll look wonderful going up the gangplank, but breathing in the clouds may prove a serious matter. Many a zipper has been unzipped at 10,000 feet.

Fashion can be outwitted.

Changes in Fashion are not as radical as they may seem, even thought her reports of the Paris collections sometimes sound as if you should actually throw out everything in your wardrobe. Actually, tying a sash high—or low—may give you the newest silhouette. As I write this book, models in my showroom are coming out beltless or with little sashes tied high under the bosom. Realistically, I know that not all women can go around beltless. If their figures can take it, perhaps their conservative tastes can't. But I assure you that if "this year's sheath" is the sheath without a belt, the woman who leaves the belt off will be the woman who looks as if she knows Fashion.

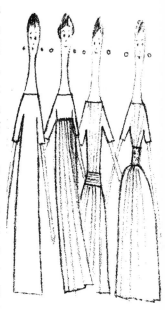

Hems, like waistlines, wander endlessly. Put this year's hem-length on last year's dress and no one will notice how old the dress is. There is always more than one silhouette in every new collection. You will naturally discard the one that you know your figure can't take, or that you don't feel at home in. But you *must* be aware of this year's hems. Do you remember the famous "New Look" of the forties when anything shorter than *long* definitely dated you? To appear in a short dress that year made people look at you as an eccentric or a country cousin from the Ozarks. That was a year when you couldn't very well outwit Fashion because it was impossible to lengthen the short dresses in your wardrobe. But it was, I think you'll agree, an exceptional year. On the whole, hemlines vary an inch or so from year to year. Yet that *one* inch longer or one inch *too* short can easily date you. Your own judgment—a stern eye on our own figure—must come into play. How short is too short? For *you*—not the girl who is modeling the dress. How long are your legs? Do muscles bulge? It is far better to look absolutely right than unharmoniously "in fashion." Hemlines can identify you as being up to the minute with the newest Paris reports, but if the up-to-the-minutes hemlines are not for you, you may enjoy being *un*fashionable.

Keep hemline straight—it's a full-time job but *very important*. Things happen to dresses that are hanging in your closets. Bias is kind to your figure but sometimes it stretches in strange directions when pressed against the grain by some well-meaning cleaner or maid.

Sometimes you can skip a complete turn in Fashion if it's

not good for you and wait for the next round—there is bound to be something both good and new for you.

The jewel in the middle of the forehead looks divine in a fashion magazine but try to wear it to the country club. Do you *want* heads to turn your way the minute you enter the room? Then be bold in your choice of line or color. But don't experiment with the very new if it is going to embarrass you. In one of my hatboxes is a single incredibly beautiful black aigrette. I have probably tried it on twenty times a year— and I've never worn it beyond my bedroom door. How different is *too* different? For me? For you?

Fashion is surprisingly sensible.

It answers not only whims, but needs. It is as new as now and often grows out of a current way of life. Most of my new ideas seem startlingly self-evident. I wonder why I didn't think of them before. "If dresses could be cut to pieces . . . ," I thought one day a long time ago. "To make packing easier— to stretch around—the top for the beach, the skirt for evening." This was the start of the piece-wardrobe that makes the major part of my collections, fills the major part of my own clothes closets, and which American women find amazingly adaptable to their busy and versatile lives. Once upon a time I used to go to Europe with a huge wardrobe trunk plus five suitcases. Today I am proud of the magic that is packed into one suitcase and a duffle bag. People will think you have lots more clothes than you really have if you stretch them around.

Most of my ideas come from trying to solve my own problems—problems just like yours. I like to be able to zip my own zippers, hook my own eyes. I need a dress that can cook a dinner and then come out and meet the guests. Don't you, too? And clothes that I can take care of without a lady's maid. And a ski suit with some sort of layer idea on top so I can take part of it off when the sun is at its hottest. My wool sweater-like dinner dress was born when I saw a shivering female in ice-blue satin at a Canadian ski resort. I like hoods because I

like my ears to be warm. And boots on a rainy day. And
bathing suits that can swim and come out of the water still
looking like bathing suits.

Sometimes times change, and what Fashion said was
good for *then* isn't good for *now*. The wartime shoulder-strap
bag is an example. It came, quite naturally, into the city in
the early forties. Every woman had more errands to do, more
carrying because deliveries were spasmodic and there were
fewer taxis on the street. It was wonderful to have two free
hands to shop with, to pull yourself on a bus or to hang on to
a subway strap. Besides, at that time, shoulders were padded
and good for holding those big straps in place.

The shoulder-strap bag had a great vogue. It was dreamed
up imaginatively in all kinds of shapes—the pouch, the pos-
tilion, the knapsack. And the important point is, it could go
to the Plaza at noon or at five or even after the theater. Today
the shoulder-strap stays in the country where it still serves
its purpose, freeing hands for the trip to the market—or to
guide the small ones to school. You seldom see it in a truly
urban setting. Somehow it has become too *emphatic* a bag.
Once it looked sophisticated and right with town clothes.
Now it either looks too military or too casual. But at the time
it arrived, it was sensible and important—and its influence
is still around. It set the pace for the duffle bag that is so useful on an airplane trip. Big bags are still sanctioned but straps
have gone down to normal holding size. You undoubtedly
have at least one really big bag in your wardrobe—but I don't
think you are wearing it on a shoulder-strap.

Fashion survives—when it deserves to.

Fashions somehow earn their right to survive. They
prove dateless because they continue to play the same role and
consequently reappear again and again. They *stay* becoming
and comfortable. With certain slight adaptations, the same
recognizable design endures long after the year of innovation.
In May 1953, the Frank Perls Gallery in Beverly Hills, Cal-
ifornia, showed an exhibit of twenty of my designs spanning

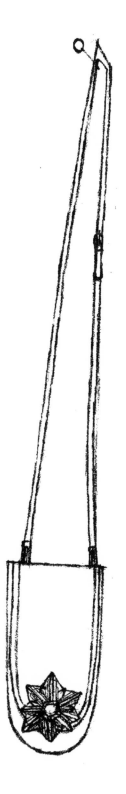

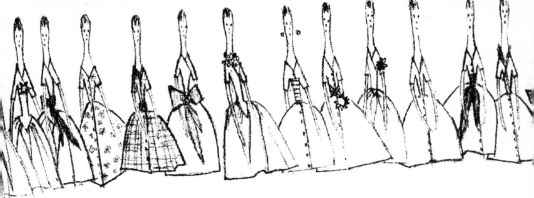

a period of twenty years—chosen because of their dateless quality. Certain basic features appeared season after season— features that grew out of my own fashion needs and way of living. The "Monastic" dress was one of them—the flowing robelike design that the wearer shaped to her own waistline with a sash or belt. The dress appeared first in 1938—yet how can I say that; it appeared hundreds of years ago—its design is classic. In '38 it had shoulder pads and was very very full. By '41 the sleeve was in one piece—a continuation of the shoulder. A few years later it had a plunging neckline; a few years more and it lost some of its fullness. And even the less-fullness began to vanish—dropped until the dress became a "String Bean" in 1950—with a belt, no less! Now it has no belt and the side pockets have moved to the hipbones. With a good little dressmaker, your 1938 "Monastic" might be made into a very up-to-date "String Bean."

Year after year the Monk's dress walks serenely through my showrooms. And because it is a serene dress, easy to wear, comfortable to live in, American women love it. And no one minds if there are a million Monk's dresses around. Our whole American tradition is based on mass acceptance of any really good idea. And besides, every woman of taste makes her dress her own. The same model may be unnoticed on one woman, unforgettable on another. It practically *never* looks like twins.

The "Popover" started as a wartime Victory Garden cover-up—moved into the house when servantless living arrived. It became a camel's hair coat, tied wrap-around style in 1948. By the summer of 1951, it played its role as dress, coat, beach wrap or hostess dress. It went over everything from evening clothes to dungarees; it could be worn as a

bathrobe or a quick something in which to answer the door-bell. The victory of the basic dress is this kind of versatility. It can be anything—everything—providing you make it a Fashion of your own. One of my Greenwich Village friends tells me that every authoress she knows "writes in a Popover." And just as each talented lady has her own writing style, each undoubtedly has her own way of looking in her "Popover." Perhaps she ties the sash with streamers in back, or knots it at one side, or winds it around and pins it with a jewel to make a girdled midriff. She may even, working on a hot summer day, wear it nightgown style with sash untied for cool comfort.

Sometimes a fashion dies overnight. What kills it? Wrong usage. Overemphasis. Something worn at the wrong time or out of place. An example is the brief flurry for gold kid in the daytime.

Gold kid had always belonged to formal evenings or perhaps an informal but dressed-up dinner party at home—never to the light of day! Suddenly Fashion decided it could move to the terrace, the cabaña, even the beach—in broad daylight! Then people got confused. They read the fashion-magazine headline that said gold kid had come out in the sunlight. They didn't read *how* and *where*. Gold belts and gold sandals began to go to the bus terminals and the office. In sidewalk settings, with city clothes, they looked garish—and therefore cheap and vulgar. But this was a blatant ignoring of what Fashion had suggested. The fault did not lie with Fashion. The women who had only half-read the gold kid story were wrong.

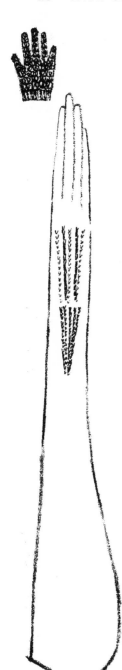

Demands of Fashion.

Fashion does not demand a submissive spirit—in fact it asks for a certain independence. The ten best-dressed women in the world, elected each year—and many of the same women reappearing year after year—will prove to you once and for all that Fashion is never a carbon copy. The ten women do not fit into any single category of age, coloring or figure type. Some are great beauties. Some are not. If there is one general observation to be made it is probably the perfection of understatement found in each wardrobe and the inspired attention to detail. So while I have said that Fashion does not demand a submissive spirit, it *does* make you aware of certain obligations. Conforming is not one of them. The more of *yourself* in your clothes, the better. *Your* imagination, your thought, *your* time, *your* energy. How you use *your* head, how you control your impulses.

You should, first of all, know the ingredients of good Fashion. You don't just settle for the first pair of white cotton gloves you find. It is the exception if you happen on a miracle. One good rule is to know before you go shopping just how many different kinds of white cotton gloves are in the stores. Newspaper ads will tell you. The fashion magazines will give you clues. A pre-picture of the glove you want gives point to your search. Short, long, buttoned, pull-on, stitched, plain, gauntlet, cuffed, textured, knit, plain. And multiply the problem of your glove purchase by every other item in your wardrobe.

Just as there are ten best-dressed women in international society, there are hundreds of sets of ten best-dressed women throughout America. "She knows clothes." "She has fashion sense." "She always looks so smart." I think a closer look will tell you that one universal statement can be made about any well-dressed woman. "She has spent time on her clothes." Not a lot of money necessarily. Not where she shops—nor whose label she wears. But time (plus energy and patience and imagination)—all her own.

The importance of you has been emphasized throughout this entire chapter. I think, if you sum up the fashion points I have tried to make, you will see that all are linked to the woman who wears the fashion. She must dress for her temperament. She must dress for her life. Physical ease is important; and even more important, mental ease. Fashion is always in the present tense. You can't lag behind. Leave the bolder untried fashions of tomorrow to the fashion leaders. And remember always that the *details* of Fashion—the variance of a hemline, the width of shoulder, where you wind your waist—all signal your awareness. Just as too much, too little, an *uncharted course* through a sea of color, or a collection of jewelry or a ready-to-wear department—will tell the world very quickly that you haven't learned what Fashion is all about.

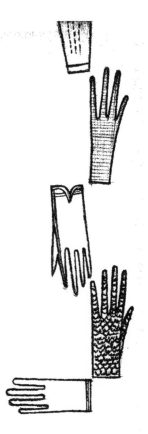

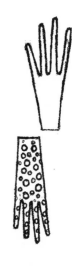

CHAPTER 2

MAKE YOUR OWN FASHION

THERE ARE THOUSANDS of you's, so you may well ask how your own particular problems can be answered by a woman who has never met you. What I hope to do is to translate my own experience with clothes, as a woman and as a designer, into universal American terms. If we take a look in my own clothes closet—one very much like yours—if we investigate my bureau drawers, my hatboxes, my shoe rack— perhaps we can proceed with some sort of order to sift and define, discard, keep, plan to add to.

Are you constantly tormented with the thought: "What shall I wear?" or with that equally famous bromide, "I have nothing to wear"? Your clothes closets are full but somehow have holes in them. No dress that is exactly right for lunch with a sophisticated mother-in-law. Nothing—but *nothing*— to wear to your husband's company picnic.

This simply means that the clothes you have chosen— beautiful and becoming as they are—don't match your life. When a designer sits down to create a new line, she begins by building imaginary portraits of the women she wants to dress. Do people really go to the country? *Can* a girl hook a trout? Can this skirt walk?

Because there are so many designers doing research on you, you can be pretty sure that somewhere there exist the exact clothes you need. And because Fashion is a mass-production business, you don't have to come to New York to find it. America's "name designers" are represented in every big department store in the country.

Your job is not so much tracking down the clothes as tracking down yourself. What one thing in your wardrobe deserves the lion's share of your Fashion dollars? Does a big evening in your life mean a dinner party in a city apartment, a suburban home, a country club? Or are big evenings bigger and scarcer—a Charity Ball, the opening of the Metropolitan, weddings, debuts? Pinpoint your major purchase first. It may be a handsome suit with lots of things to wear with it. Or the most beautifully cut golf skirt on the links. When you drive your husband to the train, is the whole community there? If you are on display, it is only sensible to be displayable.

"But what," you are going to say, "is that one major purchase going to do to my budget?"

I suggest that, in the long run, it will make your budget go further! This one wonderful purchase is going to last, not only because it is well-made, but more important, because you love it and because it is exactly right for the major occasion or the particular limelight it was bought for. Don't try to pin down a budget—so much for shoes, so much for a "good blouse." The "good blouse" may drop from heaven on a birthday —or turn up at a sale for far less than you had expected to pay. Think of a budget on a three-year basis. You may find three "lucky buys" the very first year and end up with a surplus to add to the second year's accounting. Keep a little book and write down what you buy. It will teach you *where* most of your money goes and *what* you like best; it may even help you find out *your* style. Do you love shoes? Does your notebook prove that you would rather have three pairs of shoes that you don't really need than an extra hat? Count your cashmere sweaters. Cashmere is expensive. How often do you wear a sweater and skirt? Do you like the way you look in sweaters? Perhaps, in your town, it's "the thing" to have lots of cashmere sweaters, but if you aren't really happy in them there is no reason why you shouldn't have a wardrobe of shirts and jackets. Don't give in to the temptation to spend the unexpected surplus the minute you discover it. The perfect "collector's item" may turn up the third year. How wonderful to be able to afford it!

Discover, right at the start, how many kinds of women you are expected to be. On the job. At home. At lunch. On the weekend. Fit your wardrobe to your scheme of things. You are the one who must decide how to dress your life.

Remember the old nursery riddle about Elizabeth, Lizzie, Betsy and Bess who all went together to find a bird's nest, and of course the answer was there was only one girl, not four. Can't you imagine her, living up to her various nicknames—and dressing to her different roles?

She is Elizabeth in her christening robe and when she says "I do." She's Lizzie to her friends with a super wardrobe of suits—to swim in, to ski in, to wear to work and for dates in town.

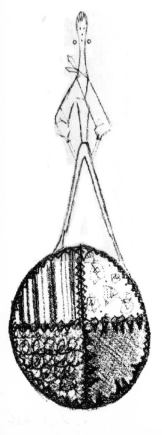

She's Betsy to her loving family—and why doesn't she get something pretty to lounge in? Vamping around the house can be the nicest tribute to a husband and family. Pants, if she has the figure. A long housecoat—gingham or calico for the country, more sophisticated stripes for city. A pretty dress-apron, to solve all kinds of indoor activities.

To Great-Aunt Bess she's Bess, a favorite niece and namesake. Tea with Great-Aunt Bess means a ladylike outfit—hat, gloves, heels. She need not wear the silk afternoon dress that used to be in everybody's wardrobe. Or the "little black dress" that you're supposed *never* to have to worry about. Life in America accepts handsome sports clothes in practically any situation. It wasn't always that way. But even Great-Aunt Bess won't frown if her niece arrives in tweeds or jersey.

The whole story of the great freedom in American clothes should perhaps be told here. Sports clothes have changed our lives—perhaps, more than anything else, made us independent women. Today's woman of fifty looks younger because the sports clothes she wears look young. Her figure is better because sports clothes demand slim figures. "Where would you wear that?" is applied more often to a ball gown than a ski suit in this day and age. We live casually, spiritedly, easily with our new-found freedom in clothes. When the Gibson Girl went swimming, she hardly dared take a stroke. How she stuck to a saddle in her monumental riding habit, I can't understand.

Suits, separates, shirtwaist dresses—smartly tailored, cut for comfort—here are clothes that should be a mainstay in *any* wardrobe. They are gifted clothes that go round the clock—round the world—with a distinguished air. Made of durable materials—good tweeds, hardy denims, corduroys, the finest wool—they live on for many seasons. Their price tags are not exorbitant. They are in tune with busy lives; commute well; look at home in the office, at the best restaurants, at the theater.

In the days of dependent women—fainting women laced to breathless beauty and hardly able to cross a street alone because of it—a sweater and skirt and bright little jacket would have been an unthinkable costume for a date with a MAN. Elizabeth Barrett took a brave step forward when she got off her couch, gave up the vapors, and ran off with Robert Browning. But still, she *floated* off, I am sure, in trailing chiffons.

The big change came in the twenties. Novelists of the time talked about it. Ernest Hemingway describes Lady Brett in *The Sun Also Rises.*

> She wore a slip-over jersey sweater and a tweed skirt, and her hair was brushed back like a boy's. She started all that.

The interesting fashion point is just where Brett wore this "look" she had started. On a brisk, breezy day at the yacht club? No. On a golf course? No. In a country setting? Anything but. At the exact moment the narrator describes he she is sitting at a bar in Paris. The time: 1926. You notice the line: "She started all this."

Other references show casual clothes moving into urban places some thirty years ago as a "new trend." Michael Arlen in *The Green Hat* notes that Iris March had her eye on the dressed-down rather than the dressed-up look. He begins his novel, published in England in the twenties, with this view of Iris:

> It has occurred to the writer to call this unimportant history *The Green Hat* because a green hat was the first thing about her that he saw: as also it was, in a way, the last thing about her that he saw. It was bright green, a sort of felt and bravely worn: being, no doubt, one of those that women who have many hats affect *pour le sport*.

And where was this casual felt hat worn? In London, at midnight, by a woman driving a Hispano-Suiza car, a very fashionable motor in that day, in that place. You notice that the author implies that only a woman with a great many hats would dare to wear this hat meant for sports outside of its proper setting. Here you have another interesting fashion point. Many trends in Fashion begin as deliberate surprises, as amusing opposites. You can be sure that Brett didn't wear a wool jersey because she was out of silk blouses. She wore it for amusement, because she liked it and felt comfortable in it. Psychologically, the world was moving toward greater freedom and independence for women everywhere. Two wars made more casual clothes seem almost a necessity. Today you don't need to be either rich or unconventional—as Brett and Iris had to be in the twenties—to dare to wear sports clothes *anywhere*.

So analyze "the times" when you analyze your wardrobe. Airplane travel with its maximum sixty pounds certainly helped to bring about a capsule wardrobe. You may not be traveling in airplanes—but you can cash in on the great advantages of a flexible co-ordinated piece-wardrobe. Steaks cooked outside—with ranch-house living moving east—certainly did a good deal to banish the tea gown. The five-day working week gave millions of people more leisure, and more

and more designers dreamed up more and more captivating
clothes to help you enjoy that leisure.

Color is a highly personal affair.

Ask yourself about color. It is probably a matter just for
you. But I suspect you can wear more variety than you think.
For years women with red hair thought they couldn't wear
pink. Fashion taught them they could and that blondes and
brunettes would eye them enviously. Invest in some dime-
store lipsticks and see what purple does—how orange be-
haves with your complexion. Color calls for experiment. You
must see it, feel its warmth, decide what it does for your skin,
your hair, your eyes.

There was a period in my life when I was afraid of color.
You are several-women-in-one in many senses. You will go
through certain phases. You will change your tastes. I had my
black-beige-brown period. Once my hair was skinned back.
Couldn't you let just a little of it cover your ears?" my mother
would say wistfully. I might have permitted a single red dress
in my wardrobe. But it had to be stark red—utterly unre-
lieved. I have come to a period in my life that is much more
fun. I have found that a so-so dress suddenly became a wonderful dress with a sash of a different color. I have discovered
the excitement of orange and pink—and of taking purple out
of the grandmother class.

Where you wear color may change your entire point of
view about it. Granted that orange and pink may be too bold
for a drawing room in mid-winter. But what about wearing
it to a resort? I am sure you would find that the two colors
fade into harmony in the Mediterranean sun.

Don't be afraid of the textile industry's version of char-
treuse, jade, emerald, olive. Now matter how vivid the
color looks, it will always be less bold than the plant, the
tree, the grass, the precious stone. You accept color in nature
as a matter of course—the vivid yellow-green of a tulip
stalk, the shiny black-green of a wall of ivy, a blue-green

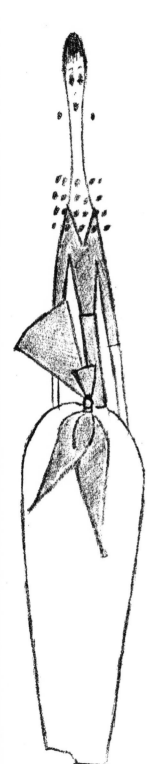

pine, a gray-green willow. Color in your wardrobe need not be difficult and it will give you and your audience a great deal of pleasure.

Take advantage of *where* you are going to wear it. If you go to Venice where the sea is the color of the scene, be sure to bring a wardrobe of blues and greens along. Or deliberately wear dark red because it looks lovely with turquoise. If you are a skier, remember that you will be silhouetted against a snow-white background. Black is probably the most dramatic color you choose in this pure-white setting but any strong bright color will also be exciting.

Color doesn't have to cost money.

Color is, perhaps, the most imaginative touch you can afford. Fine lines cost money. And so do luxurious fabrics and the names of great designers. Color doesn't have to. And it is true metamorphosis because it creates an immediate and visible change. Your friends are used to you in navy blue. They hardly look twice. But if navy blue changes to turquoise, you can be certain it will be noticed.

Color changes its spots.

Texture affects color. Turquoise in satin and turquoise in jersey are two entirely different stories. In a shiny fabric, a color may be too bright, too hard, to live up to. In a dull fabric it is softer, may seem an entirely different color even though it has been put into the same dye pot. The satin that looks garish in a whole dress may be very interesting used in touches—a string tie belt, piping on the edge of a pocket or around the neckline. How much, how little—this is especially important if you decide to try color, and when you decide on color think of it in terms of the fabric. Don't just go looking for a dress that is pink. Remember that pink is better in some fabrics—perhaps too pink in others.

The overwhelming importance of fit.

I know an attractive woman who is blessed with a slender figure but somehow she always looked drowned in her clothes. Suddenly she discovered *fit*. Everything came blessedly into proportion. From shapeless, she went to *shape*—yet she was still buying the same size. How can this happen? In the past she had simply walked into size 12 and expected it to fit her everywhere. But it didn't. Just because you can get into a size 12, *don't* think it means you are a *perfect* size 12. Few women are. You may be a size 12 in the hips and bust—but not in the shoulders and waist, or vice versa. Perhaps a size 10 will fit you *except* in the waist. The waist alteration is cheaper than trying to reduce a larger size to correct over-all measurements. So if the size 10 has good seams, take it in preference to the size 12. Only if a size 12 fits you *everywhere*, will you *look* and *feel* like a size 12. And certainly because half the success of a fashion depends on how it fits, you must understand the adjustments that your figure asks for.

One of the big problems in mass production is how to make all clothes fit all sizes and shapes of females. It can't be done, so more and more categories of sizes have been added, with the hope that one or another's designer's line will answer one or another woman's problem. No woman can expect to ask for the size she thinks she is in *all* lines or in *all* categories.

The government is responsible for the standardization of sizes and a noble effort has been made to make things easier for you when you go into a store to buy a dress. During World War II, it was possible to do a real research job on the sizes and shapes of women in America. The WACS and the WAVES, women from every state in the Union, were representative in every way except age group.

But immediately, a flaw creeps in. The woman who is size 12 at twenty may not be size 12 at forty; but because she has changed in width *only*, size 14 will still be too big for her

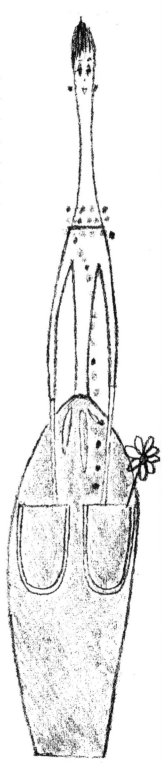

over-all proportions. This is the explanation of half-sizes, designed for more mature women. Junior sizes, like half sizes, are designed for an age group. They are identified by off numbers: 7, 9, 11, 13, 15. They have a junior look—short-waisted, usually fuller skirts, young fashions in the sleeves, the puffed sleeve for instance. They say *type* just as half sizes say *type*. Junior *is* young. Half size *is* mature. Two categories, added in recent years, solve the problem for the very tall and the very short. Brief (sometimes called 5 ft. 3 and under) is scaled down in every way to height. Within the brief range are sizes by number to take care of width. Tall does the same thing for the woman who stands taller than 5 ft. 6.

Most of you—government statistic show this—fall into the general group known as misses, identified by even numbers: 8, 10, 12, 14, 16, 18, 20. Neither half sizes nor junior sizes will solve your problem, because the *style* of the dress may be all wrong. At 30 you may not want puffed sleeves, a high-waisted look. On the other hand you don't want the extreme conservatism that often marks the half-size line. That is why I have said it is up to you to understand *where* adjustments must be made—because some alteration is inevitable in most cases.

There is still another consideration. Designers are human beings—they are apt to design clothes that *they* like. I am 5 feet 7 inches tall. Some of my clothes *would* drown smaller women. You will find, with a little research on your own, that certain designers are "for *you*." The designer that specializes in the straight skirt, the all-over slim look, the way, perhaps you want to look, poses another problem. Are you willing to submit to the underpinnings that this designer's clothes make imperative? I have heard some women say, proudly, that they can exchange clothes with their sixteen-year-old daughters. This is a very revealing remark. Does it mean that a woman over forty is wearing a fashion that tells the world she has forgotten she is no longer in her teens? Ask yourself this question: "Do I want clothes for the age I am— the age I look—the age I want to look?"

To sum up—you may approach this problem of fit in several ways. I suggest the following, in the order I would choose if I were you. First: *look* at your figure. You know if you're too fat. Consult your doctor and find out how much you can lose safely. He will be only too glad to help you and if you are really overweight he will disapprove from the standpoint of health. Your figure is adjustable—through diet and exercise. Instead of struggling from one size to another, you will save time and frustration, by banishing potatoes. But be realistic. Reducing won't guarantee a perfect figure if your bones aren't arranged that way. Accept the fact that some alterations will be necessary in whatever you buy. Hem length, for instance. The fitter at the store will indicate where alterations are necessary and you will certainly save money if you can either do the alterations yourself or find a little dressmaker. Accept the fact that you will probably need some sort of support underneath. I don't mean foundations that push you out of any resemblance to the way nature made you. A part of the beauty of clothes is the freedom I've talked so much about. The girdle that ruins your muscular balance will also destroy the grace of the dress. But clothes—the right ones—through shape and fit, can make you look a lot more ideal than you really are. And finally, it is true that better dresses (which means spending a little more for them) usually offer you bigger seams to let out, more hem to let down, so you may stay in the size that is in correct proportion for your height, and cheat a little at the hipline, waistline, bosom, when your widths don't quite comply with the standardized width measurements. The important thing to remember is that fit can *make* a look—or ruin it.

Finding the designer who seems to be designing exactly for you is not difficult. Look at fashion magazines and memorize the names of the designers who seem to like the shapes you like. You will find that a picture does not always tell the truth about the exact shape. The dress may turn out to be too full in the skirt—too short in the waist. But if you ask the salesgirl for a "name designer," she will be glad to bring you

the clothes she has from that line. In one or two seasons, you can find out which designer seems consistently to have *your* shape in mind. When you try on the dress, don't underestimate the power of the three-way mirror that most fitting rooms are equipped with. It won't forget your back—and people *do* see you both coming and going.

YOUR OWN COLLECTIONS

I know all the hazards of keeping things. I remember the story of the Frenchwoman who had a box labeled "Bits of String Too Short for Any Good Use." But I still believe firmly that any woman who loves clothes is going to be a collector. She will make her own mixture by instinct. Certain clothes will stay in her wardrobe for years. Mistakes—there are bound to be some—will be quickly eliminated. The fashion for *you* is so much a part of you that you can easily tell when you've made a mistake. Did your new beau send you an orchid when you really like daisies? Then there must have been something wrong with that new dress you bought!

You will bless the ageless clothes in your collection. They are the backbone of any closet . . . things you can depend upon when you need them. Always wear something old with something new for balance. Often it is the "big major purchase" I spoke of at the start of the chapter. Sometimes it is the "lucky find"—or the "collector's item." I think at once of the farm sweater I picked up in a marketplace years ago— and the pleated nightgown from Italy that is as beautiful as the day I found it—and the peasant cape that is rugged and enduring.

In the next few chapters I am going to talk about my own mixtures, from big purchases to small ones, starting, I think, *with* the small ones because the sash—the beads—the pin you wear with a dress may be the one thing that makes the dress unforgettably yours. There can be no Fashion unless shape, color, texture, fit are exactly right for you.

CHAPTER 3

YOUR COLLECTION
OF LITTLE THINGS

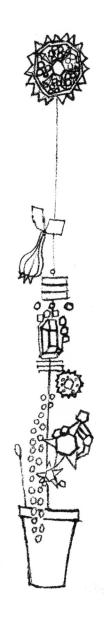

JEWELRY, BELTS, SHOES, gloves, bags, hats, scarves—
these are the biggest little projects in your wardrobe.
They are signatures of your special tastes, clues to the kind
of woman you like being. Each is an idea in itself and you
will quickly learn that you can't wear too many ideas at the
same time.

If an insurance appraiser looked at my collection, the first
thing he would discover is that I have no *real* jewelry in my
life. Money is not the determining factor in the kind of
jewelry I like. There are some women who would rather give
up a part-time maid or a whole-time cook for an all-time diamond. Diamonds are a taste. Just as emeralds are—and rubies
and star sapphires and real pearls. They are what an appraiser
would call "precious"—and *perhaps* a girl's best friend if she
is interested in intrinsic value.

I am much more interested in the Fashion value of
jewelry, and Tiffany would label my collection junk. But to
me it is very special junk that I have been collecting, piece by
piece, from Woolworth's, from Austria, from attics, from
antique shops—and from the time I was given my first spending money. Your taste in jewelry may not be my taste at all.
It doesn't matter. The point I am making is *collect*—and
keep—and make each piece your own. What you collect will
depend on you.

You may settle on three or four very valuable identification pieces. I think immediately of my friend and her crown
pin of important diamonds—worn as consistently with her

country jerseys as with her evening clothes. Or you may decide, as I have, that there's more fun in finding jewelry that spells Fashion instead of finance.

MY OWN COLLECTION
From Austria:

The big pin, this one dimensional, looking like a mass of delicately woven wire. The correct term, I guess, is filigree— but filigree always sounds to me like ornate and old-fashioned lace. This pin doesn't look old-fashioned. It might have been turned out by precision machinery with its intricate windings of thin gold and silver threads, the gold very pale, the silver whitish. I saw it, liked it, bought it—for not very much money. I enjoy being identified with it and people often mention it. I wear it hear and there—on the collar of a silk shirt, on the belt of a dinner dress, with a chain looped through it, to hold down a deep-V neckline that wouldn't fit otherwise.

From the attic:

The pin made from a miniature of my great-grandfather looking Abraham Lincolnish. The frame is very simple gold, kind of dented. The corner jeweller attended to the business of the safety clasp. If I want it talked about I surround it with old-fashioned stickpins and chains. Just as often it is used to fade into the color of a dress, looking like a dark jewel.

Hungarian bracelet:

Silver washed with gold and the gold beginning to wear off which makes it more attractive. When a link broke and I had to take it to a repair shop, my firm instructions were: "DON'T POLISH IT OR DIP IT IN A GOLD WASH." I like gold to look old. I like brass if it's dull, looking like old gold. Brass doesn't have to look brassy.

Color in beads:

I've always had a few colored beads in my collection—
lately I've added more. They were added to my collection to
go with certain clothes—to link with the color—to serve as
an extra color. I like the green glass ones, rather small, with
gold gadgets in between—there are several strands, some add
another color. If I mix them up properly they look like something they aren't.

Silver dagger:

Dirty on purpose so the silver won't gleam, definite in
design and quite dashing pinned to a belt, a sash, a pocket, a
lapel.

Rhinestone and paste department:

If the glitter doesn't try to look like the real thing—it's
good. I pass it by if it tries to imitate diamonds. But big—
bold—gaudy on purpose—it's fun.

Beautiful bargain:

I went looking for rose diamonds and found the perfect
pin for $200. I kept on looking and found an old pin with
pieces of glass—knocked around and dusty enough to look
like rose diamonds—and bought it for $30.

Pincushion looking like a porcupine:

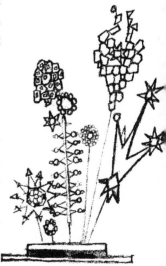

It bristles with my minor extravagances—hat pins, stickpins, sensible pins, even the dressmaker variety. It always
reminds me of the old rhyme—"See a pin, pick it up, all the
day you'll have good luck." And I probably *would* pick it up
because my life simply couldn't go without pins. I don't use
them to be practical or to hide my sins. (No broken shoulder

straps operating on a pin.) I use them boldly, on purpose, where they're meant to be seen. And they can *really* be that lucky piece if you get tangled up in scarves.

Hairpins acting like jewelry:

Because I have long hair I am the perfect target for hair-pins. All my friends send them to me: big gold ones, little gold ones, tortoise shell, silver, leather-covered for tweeds, and high ones to let things dangle from for evening. Hearts, for instance. Or stars or pearls. Sometimes months go by without one of them leaving the bureau or pincushion but they are as much a part of my permanent collection as the plain gold marriage band on my finger.

Case of the disappearing pearl bib— and its satisfying reappearance:

If you can't figure your way out of a bad purchase, get rid of it. That's axiomatic. But if you have spent money on some-thing and found it's all wrong, take a second look before you discard it. A perfect example is my famous pearl bib. It looked wonderful in the showcase. And all the fashion magazines had been talking about it. Besides it was ON SALE. I couldn't wait to get it home to try it with the right clothes. After an hour of struggling in and out of all the clothes I own, I faced the fact that *if* the pearl bib was *right*, then my entire wardrobe was *wrong*. The pearl bib gave me, candidly, the "Theda Bara Look." And that "look," if my memory serves me, was somewhere back around 1915. The first blow was the two little words "On Sale." Which meant nonreturnable. So here I was—stuck—with my "Theda Bara Look." Or was I? I took a second look and thought: "Here are a lot of awfully pretty pearls." They ranged in size and in lengths. After I put on my glasses I saw that it wasn't going to be too hard to sep-arate the strands from the bib. I hadn't made a bad purchase after all. I had made one of the most wonderful purchases of

my entire life. I had acquired a whole pearl wardrobe—
chokers, one-stranders, two-stranders, a really long length.
And some left over for bracelets.

TIPS TO COLLECTORS
How much at one time:

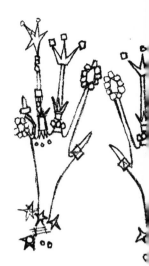

The pearl bib story immediately makes me think of how
many *things* I put around my neck every morning when I dress.
I'm tall, and several strands of gold chain, each one dangling
its specialty, aren't going to foreshorten me. But if you are not
very tall—and your object is to look taller—be careful about
the amount of jewelry worn at the top. I like to mix gold
chains and pearls as every woman does. But I also like to vary
the mixture—gold chains with pins, with colored beads,
with a simple black choker made of highly polished wooden
links, with a shoelace or a piece of ribbon tied around my
neck to pin things to. The first function of jewelry is to be
decorative—but it does have other functions. It can call
attention *to* or distract attention *from*. Women with beautiful
hands may decide to wear exquisite rings—or they may
decide to wear a simple band and let the beauty of their hands
stand alone. Certainly the way your ears are formed will
decide what kinds of earrings you buy.

Work up to effects:

If you admire the way a woman looks wearing five gold
chains and there haven't been any gold chains in your life,
don't go out and buy five gold chains all at once. Work up to
the effect you want gradually. Buy one chain, perhaps two.
Try them together. Try them with a string of beads added.
Increase until the effect is right for you. Remember that your
height, the shape of your face, the length of your neck, the
width of your shoulders, will all enter into the question of
how much or how little.

Plan to keep what you buy:

The whole basis of a collection is keeping it. If you plan
to keep what you buy you will be less apt to go overboard
and buy something for the moment. You will, of course, go
through stages as a person. Like every woman in the world,
after your first trip to Santa Fe, you are going to have a
turquoise and silver period. You may love Santa Fe and all it
stands for so much that you will wear turquoise and silver
the rest of your life. You may completely outgrow silver beads
and rows and rows of narrow silver bracelets. But don't
throw them away. In your more sophisticated city role, you
may still want a whole armful of bracelets. And what about
narrow gold interspersed with narrow silver for a coat-of-
mail effect. Granted the turquoise ring you bought when you
went West for your vacation is much too Indian-y now that
you are working in New York. But this is an exception. The
simple silver beads are still charming with a black cashmere
sweater. Unless you *know* something is never going to be worn
again, keep it.

Have things made:

Little leather bracelets, for instance, tailored by the cob-
bler around the corner. Yes, he *may* raise his eyebrows or
shrug his shoulders—but he will be just as pleased as you are
when you show him how a narrow strip of leather, with delicate saddle stitching and a tiny buckle, becomes the perfect
bracelet for a certain tweed suit. Go to shops in the garment
district where beads and sequins and hooks and eyes and buttons and buckles are sold to the trade. Assemble your own
string of beads, like no other strand of beads in the world,
because you have mixed and matched to the colors in your
wardrobe. I used to design jewelry by the sketchbook
method; now I go straight to the factory and pick and choose
from hundreds of trays of beads. Right now, I like big balls

of color to *belong* to a certain dress, a certain neckline. But that's today. Perhaps by the time you are reading this book, I shall have found another way to decorate a neckline, because there are endless things that can double as jewelry. Buckles, buttons, interesting fastenings.

Certain women may want very personal things in their collection: golf medals, the gold chain a grandfather gave a grandmother, a horsehair bracelet found in an old trunk. Other women may want the jewelry the fashion magazines report (and they do a fine job, often inventing a whole new way with colored stones). Whether you add to your collection from Cartier or the attic, think twice before you admit the piece to your collection. Does it look as if it belonged to your kind of clothes, your kind of taste? If you have learned to use jewelry as a fashion point, you will wear the same piece over and over again. Do you *want* to be identified with it? I can think of five women I know who this very moment may very well be putting on or taking off the piece of jewelry that is theirs alone. Each piece is a distinguished fashion in its own right.

The jeweled bird pin:

An heirloom and valuable enough to be insured. From a French grandmother of great elegance. Worn in Paris a century ago with taffeta and lace. Worn by the smart young great-great-granddaughter on the lapel of her gray flannel suit.

The little silver ball studded with fake jewels:

It, too, came from the Rue de Rivoli but it's not valuable at all. It was a lapel pin originally. The owner had a small ring attached and it is her one and only dangle on a bracelet of baroque pearls. The little jewelled ball may turn up on some other lapel, but only the woman who took the trouble to take it to a jeweler will wear it as a dangle.

The big bold piece of glass:

Bound in a thin solid rim of gold, looking like something stolen from the Crown Jewels. Worn by the girl with her hair skinned back, always hatless. She pins it to the cocoon-shaped coats she likes, buttonless, so they need a pin to hold both sides together. She was lucky enough to find the original Lanvin "cocoon" on a sales rack. She made it hers. Had it copied in different colors. Always the identical pin fastens it.

The watch-ring:

It's mine. I need it because I like to be on time. I chose it because a wrist watch interferes with my bracelets. And a watch pinned on a dress never seems to be looking at you from the right place.

The medals that don't dangle:

With three gold medals to cope with, the lady wisely decided she looked weighted down if they hung from her bracelet (you can drown—quite literally—if you're wearing too much.) She designed a new bracelet from a new watch chain, using the medals as links.

Traditional jewelry designs:

Star, cross, teardrop pendant, a cameo, a lavaliere, a medallion, a crown, a snowflake—and on and on. Some are associated with periods in history, with foreign governments, with certain regions, with ancient symbols. Sometimes yesterday's jewelry loses the look of the past and becomes tomorrow. A spirited diamond of many carats and great fire is inherited, complete with prongs. All you can really *see* is the prongs. I know of one such diamond. It is now the highpoint of a modernistic ring, built in a twisted-rope effect, as dramatically dimensional as today. I am not sure I like it, but it is unforgettable and a perfect example of how today can become tomorrow.

Another example is the gold chain made of yellow beads, each with many flat planes and Napoleonic stars cut out in each plane. The original Empire piece had an old-fashioned locket attached to it and looked like great-grandmother. The twentieth-century lady who wears it has removed the locket; all you see now is beads with stars—making a highly sophisticated modern chain.

Stickpins and cuff links:

The usually belong to a man's collection of yesterday's jewelry. They were originally either gifts for important occasions or the affectations of dandies—so they weren't cheap to start with. But because they have little value for today's man (except in the French cuff set) almost any antique store can offer you trays and trays to choose from. My red pincushion (and my cuff-link box) are evidence of the bargains and the fun you can have if you decide to collect. I use the pins to anchor a scarf, adorn a lapel, stick in a hat. The cuff links bejewel a cuff or are transformed into pins or earrings.

Earrings, an individual affair:

Certain women feel undressed without them. Others say they hurt—or fall off—and are too much trouble because part of the pair is always missing. In an increasingly hatless society, earrings play an important role because they give you a dressed-up look at the top to harmonize with with your long gloves, your cocktail-hour shoes. But I can't agree with certain fashion authorities who feel that the truly smart woman is rarely seen without earrings.

Wearing earrings is a little like driving a car—it's easier if you've started young. I can sympathize with one of my

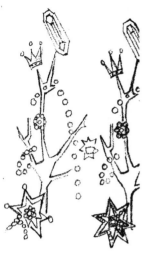

friends who sighs, "I *had* to have a feather fan for the Junior Prom in 1922, but nobody even thought of earrings." She tries them on today, feels uncomfortable, invariably tucks them into her evening bag before the night is over. Here is another case of trying to live up to Fashion for Fashion's sake. It can't be done. If you don't feel at home with a fashion avoid it. I know women who can't tie a scarf—women who always manage to stick themselves with hat pins or stickpins—women who literally handcuff themselves when dangling baubles catch in a sweater sleeve. Because they don't know how to tie a bow, can't avoid stabbing themselves—certain departments of Fashion are not for them. But remember, you miss half the fun if you have to banish certain things from your wardrobe.

How much jewelry?

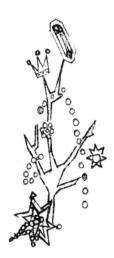

That is a question you alone can answer. I give you fair warning. Jewelry *can* get you talked about. "She looks like a Christmas tree." "All those diamonds are vulgar." "If you call a birdcage hanging on your wrist *Fashion!*" *Who* is talking? Does it matter to *you* what they're saying? *Where* are you wearing the pin that glitters, the wealth of rings? Think of the person you are expected to be in the community. What do your husband and child expect of you? Will they misunderstand hearts in your hair? If they will, give up this particular Fashion fun. Let them keep on thinking of you as a serene background—not a frightful experience.

And Fashion *does* help you to decide. Editors with great taste give an official okay to lots and lot of jewelry, provided it's banked at the wrist or massed at the neckline. What they don't okay are oddities—an ankle bracelet worn under sheer stockings. On the other hand, if you have lovely ankles, why not wear a big bold slave bracelet affair at the beach. But this is fun—*not* fashion.

Jewelry and the brand-new dress:

How can you make a dress that feels too new feel as if it suddenly belongs to you? Practicing a dress around the house is a fine idea—but I've discovered something even better. Go straight to your jewelry collection and try on your favorite pieces—*then* look in the mirror at you in your new dress. You will be instantly reassured. The dress has lost its too-new look. Familiar gold or pearls or family heirlooms have softened it, made it look like you—and you can't wait to wear it to the party!

BELTS AND SASHES

Belt drawer:

This is a big drawer, and an important one. I often stand in front of it for a full five minutes deciding what's going around my middle today. By now you know that I like buttons to button, buckles to buckle, sashes to tie—and also that I like things to wind around in different ways to make different waistlines. This should give you some clue as to what you will find in the belt drawer. Here is an old tired piece of velvet, rather mouse-colored—but it has softness, elegance. It is a sewed belt from a dress I once owned. It's a girdle-belt with a tucked look. It fastens with a row of hooks and eyes, the way French clothes are made. I haven't found anything to wear with it *yet*, but some day I will. So I keep it. It's so perfect in itself, that I must get around very soon to hunt for a dress to go with it. If you see a belt that is wonderful in itself—buy it. Then go out and get a dress to put it on. This is naturally not for all belts. Many will serve you day in and day out on all types of clothes. But if the belt is a fashion in itself, let it *be* the fashion point of your costume. A really important belt is cousin to a really dramatic piece of jewelry.

HOW TO TAME A SCARF—A SASH—A BOW

It all takes practice, but when you've learned how it's pure delight. Visualize the figures above without their identifying scarf or sash or bow. What you would have is a paper-doll row of identical twins like the ones you used to cut out of

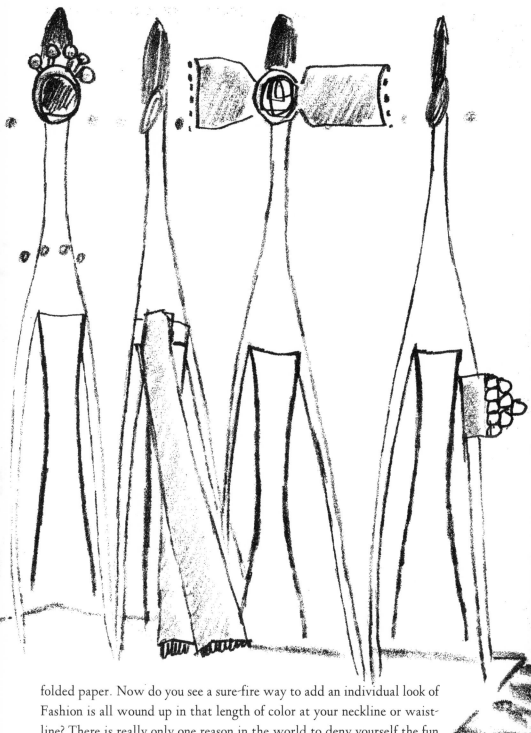

folded paper. Now do you see a sure-fire way to add an individual look of Fashion is all wound up in that length of color at your neckline or waist-line? There is really only one reason in the world to deny yourself the fun of these Fashion extras: that you can't learn to tame them. But you can.

Joys of a sash belt:

Let's define a sash as anything that ties. It can be narrow black velvet ribbon or bias-cut jersey or spaghetti-strings. Many of the clothes I design have sashes attached to the dress, in the front or at the sides, asking for tying. Many of my dresses are an incomplete design *without* the sash, even if it is a separate. I use sashes to achieve variations in a waistline and for comfortable adjustment. Tie a sash high and the style becomes Empire; tie it at your natural waistline for American Contemporary; tie it low for the recaptured and revamped look of the twenties.

I also use sashes for a color note. They may match, blend or accent by contrast. Remember that an identical color in a different texture and fabric will give the effect of a different hue. Thus a one-color outfit my create an effect of more than one color.

The advantages of sash belts are endless. You can make them yourself. You can choose material that will *cling* as no leather belt will ever cling. You can create illusions about a waistline that may not be in perfect proportion to the rest of your figure. If you are going to make a sash belt, your choice of material is the most important factor in the success of the belt. A sash to some of you will conjure up immediately a picture of your first party dress with the stiff taffeta bow in the back. This is exactly what *my* sash belt *isn't*. It is based on the traditional girdle-belt worn in ancient Greece. It resembles the Japanese kimono sash. You are perfectly familiar with it in your sophisticated world. It ties raincoats, polo coats, leather jackets, bathrobes. It is found less often in dresses and suits.

Wool jersey, cotton and elastic cloth are the best materials to make a belt that will cling. Satin is soft to look at but too slippery to tie you in and stay put. Fur will cling but it won't tie very well. Felt makes a good contour belt— not a sash belt that sticks. Rope is all right but doesn't really convey a sash idea.

The most perfect sash belt in my drawer was tracked down in a Basque marketplace. It is made of coarsely woven pink cotton, fringed at the ends. It winds and sticks and clings and can be pulled in like an honest-to-goodness girdle. My second-best is a home-made version of the elastic cloth belt. Do you remember when elastic cloth first made its appearance in the cinch belt? It was a revolutionary idea and a good one. But the initial elastic belt and the one that is still around in department stores is buckled or hooked. It is *not* a tieable sash—and somehow looks a little like a big garter. The advantages of elastic cloth are its expandability and its snugness—there is no size worry. And it certainly pulls your waist *in*. My objections to it in its ready-made state are aesthetic. To me, there is something stiff—well, *garterish*—about it. My solution has been to buy elastic cloth, either narrow or wide, usually in dead black. Elastic cloth *tied* somehow doesn't look like elastic anymore and it retains all of the virtues of the manufacturer's elastic belt—it clings, it sticks, it pulls your waist in. (Note: narrow elastic also makes bracelets or neckbands or ties—to pin things on.)

You miss all the fun if you can't tie things:

Sashes, veils, string ties, scarves—do they lie idle in your bureau drawers because you can't handle them? I pick my models for their figures, their walk, their shining hair. Not for their ability to tie a bow. But because most of my clothes have something to tie somewhere, every showing means a foreshortened lunch hour for me. I have to be right on hand to act like a dresser in the theater. If you really care about Fashion, sit down right now and *learn to tie*. An ascot, a bandanna, a neckband, a bowknot. This means knowing how to fold first, knowing how to loop next, knowing how to get the knot straight, knowing how to make the ends even—or uneven—on purpose.

Beau Brummel would know what I am talking about. When he tied his stocks, his rule was perfection on the first

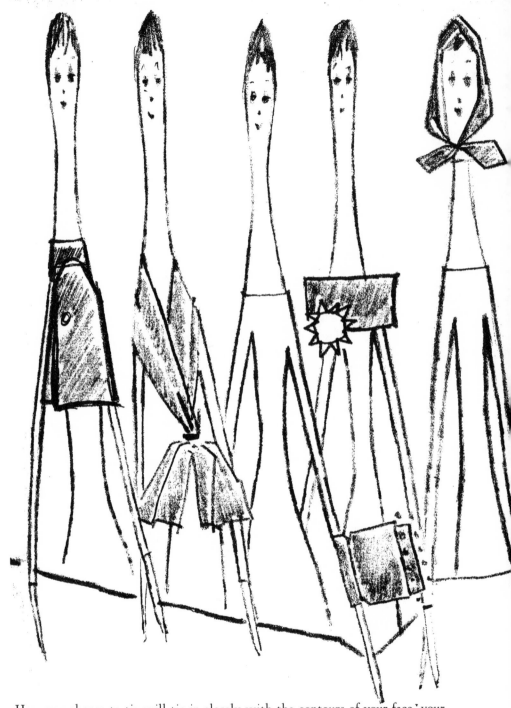

How you choose to tie will tie in closely with the contours of your face, your figure—and will reflect your taste and temperament as well. The kitten bow may not be for you, either because nature made you round or because it seems all wrong for the tailored look you like. So experiment—with spaghetti strings, with sashes that loop at the side and trail, with a bow that rivals the white-tie technique

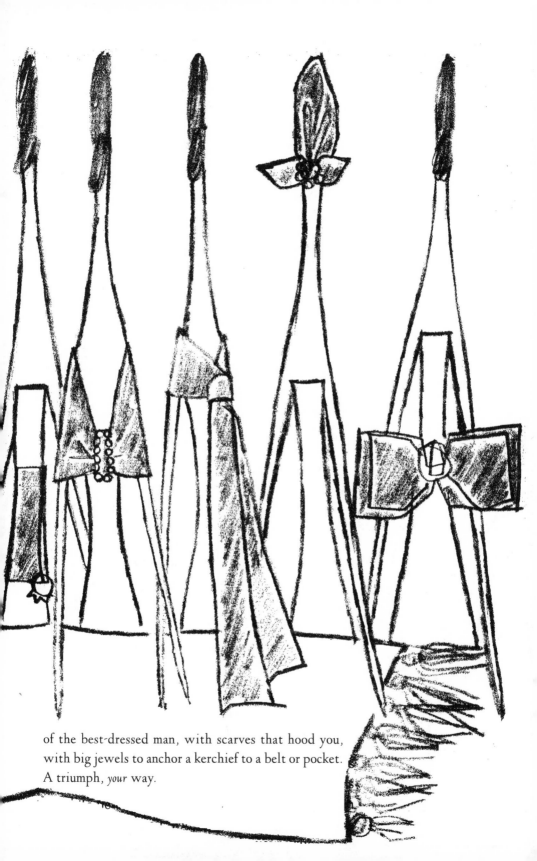

of the best-dressed man, with scarves that hood you,
with big jewels to anchor a kerchief to a belt or pocket.
A triumph, *your* way.

try. If something went wrong, the scarf was tossed into the laundry to be rewashed, repressed. Obviously this isn't always practical. But the man who had the reputation of the best-dressed man in the England of his time would have told you flatly: "No starched fabric can ever be retied and look right."

What width belt?

Your waist and the belt, *your way* with the belt—these are determining factors. I cannot generalize. I cannot chart your waistline. "Size 12, 110 lbs. —may you wear a wide belt?" I think at once of the woman who is size 12, 110 lbs. who has found she can wear nothing but narrow belts. The measuring-tape truth of her is this: her waistline is 27 inches; her hips are small, bust medium—adding up to a square look. A wide belt makes her look *more* square.

Fun of strings:

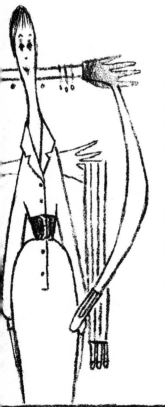

An Italian woman in my workroom named them "spaghetti." They are my favorite string belts, worn two or three at a time, wound round and round—high, low, criss-crossed—wherever you want them. They are made from narrow strips of material cut on the bias, sewed like piping. Wonderful in wool-jersey or silk-satin. Decorative, because they seem to keep the dress in motion—and I like clothes to look alive. I often stitch string belts to a dress just under the bosom, hoping the wearer will tie it high Princess or Empire style or cross and recross in the Grecian way. But if you want to undo the stitching and settle for a row of spaghetti at your normal waistline it's still "Fashion."

The good leather belt:

One at least. More if you can afford it. Classic leather, usually medium width, conventionally buckled. Pigskin and calfskin in good tawny colors are wearable with the major part of your wardrobe. Brass buckles, saddle stitching, ornamental fastenings and dangles may limit the versatility of the belt. All are fine in their place but they designate, and the belt maybe too important in interest. If you can afford lots of belts, add patent leather, alligator, colored leathers, suede, velvet, fur. Remember that suede begins to look shabby quite soon, especially around the buckle. Fur belts have served me well. The one that is some sort of cow or pony, white with tannish markings, is a stand-by. The one of silky black galyak is a nice shiny contrast for black broadcloth; I like it with restaurant suits. The leopard turned out to be doing double duty in a hatbox—I'd put it there when I began to brood about changing hatbands.

Color in belts:

It's good if it's sharp and the rest of the belt is simple in design. I like my shiny yellow leather one. It has holes in it, rimmed with brass (like the holes in a sail for the ropes to go through.) Brass is there, but it is used more discreetly than if it were a whole buckle or a nailhead design. Narrow leather belts in color often set off the print in a dress and become part of the pattern. A safe rule is to know what you are going to wear the colored belt *with*. Don't just go out and buy a red belt because you like red, *unless* it is the red belt you have decided to built a whole costume around.

Advantages of contour belts:

They take care of your waistline faults if they are really contoured to your waist. Safest thing is to design your own shaped belt, dipping it slightly in back to make it cling, narrowing or widening where you need to for perfect fit. Then take fabrics or leather matching definite clothes and have a belt wardrobe made to order. The shoe man will help, or the little dressmaker, or your own sewing machine. In the end

you'll save money. Just for fun start checking how many belts you own. How many do you really *wear*?

SHOES

Can you walk with him?

Think of it. When you buy shoes you are not just buying for your own feet. You are buying for your husband's tastes, for the things you are going to walk to. Does he take big steps? Would he rather help poor delicate little you into a taxi? Your shoe wardrobe, as you see, is far more than keeping your feet on the ground. If there is an outdoor man in your life, don't annoy him by getting a blister when you follow him in a golf tournament. If you have a taxi-lover in your home, be sure you have plenty of spindly heels to give him an excuse to *take* a taxi. Think of it: *your* shoes can soothe *his* conscience.

Known by your shoes:

That's what people used to say about a lady. And it still holds true. An ankle strap, a buckle at the wrong time of day, something too shiny trimming your pump—like too much jewelry in the wrong place—it *can* make you misunderstood.

Enough shoes:

It is not extravagant to have extra pairs of shoes, often an exact duplicate of a model you know fits well. The object is not to have shoes in *all* colors, in *all kinds* of leather; that might conceivably *be* an extravagance. The purpose is practical: to get more mileage per pair from shoes you know are comfortable—keeping your feet healthy and happy at the same time. For healthy feet: change your shoes at least twice a day and never wear the same pair of shoes day after day in succession. A variety of heel heights will actually strengthen your arches. Some feet cannot wear a three-inch heel. Some feet cannot wear shoes that are absolutely heelless. But consider changes *within your range.*

I prefer a low-slung, shaped heel, that looks higher than Cuban but isn't. The illusion of height lies in the inside curve of the heel. So, in the mood, the shoe is dressy; in practice it's sensible. There was a time when low heels were associated with schoolgirls, nurses, teachers and social workers. You can be grateful that all that's a memory. When I first put models in my showrooms in low heels, the buyers were scandalized. "A cocktail dress with heels like that!" I found nobody was looking at the clothes, so I hustled the models into spikes. Several seasons later I was able to restore low heels. The trend had become an established fashion.

My own shoe collection:

And more important, how I assembled it. First I decided on heel height—for *my* feet, *my* tastes—and for day, for night, for home and on the job. My heel height, as I have told you, is in the lower range—from no-heel to a moderate two inches at most. Do you like heels as heels? I do, so I vary them. I like built-up wooden heels, shaped heels, and *no* heels. Lack of heel can be heel interest in itself, calling attention to your own nature-shaped heel and how it rests on the leather sole. Do you like your own toes well enough to have them show? Indeed, are you *proud* of showing them? For a long time Fashion frowned at open toes and sling backs. But women said "Why . . . they're comfortable." So Fashion went to work and said: "Very well, be really open, show all your toes as nature made them." With ten straight well-pedicured toes decoratively strapped in a sandal, open toes look pretty. But if one toe overlaps, or curls under, the fashion is *not* for you. I like closed toes—the classic pump, pointed tow, cut low, and my own version of the little heel. I have this shoe in black kid, in black fur, in fabric, and my all-time favorite, light tawny suede. But I also have open sandals, gillies, the moccasin, boots and their opposite—the naked thong shoe that feels like no shoe at all.

Do you remember the days when every autumn meant a new pair of black suede pumps, and a pair of brown ones if you could afford it? Today, there is very little standardization. Shoes are an individual affair. Fashion says is it is all right to wear black shoes with a brown suit or with navy blue. The shape of the shoe in relation to the shape of your foot and the silhouette you are wearing is the determining factor. Still, there are some rules. Satin has not yet taken to the street. We've had fabric shoes, straw shoes—even plastic which seems vulgar to some but as charming as a Cinderella slipper to others. Perhaps what you should look for is soft construction in shoes—it's cropping up everywhere.

The shoe that's yours alone:

I know one woman who has red heels on every shoe in her wardrobe. Put on specially, of course. I know another who has the same Perugia model, circa 1949, recopied every year. Seventh Avenue and visiting buyers will tell you that my models are almost universally dressed in my favorite low-slung pump in tawny suede, or in next-to-nothing sandals. Many a woman would rather go without a new dress for a not-so-extravagant pair of custom-made shoes—done just for her, in the design and color and material she asks for. Think about it.

I've done things to ready-made shoes to make them mine. The black pump that came with a black lacquered heel. Too shiny. I scraped off the lacquer and came down to white wood—liked it a lot better that way.

Banish shoe mistakes:

If a shoe hurts, give it away. A fashionable foot is not worth it if it hurts. But is it always discomfort? It may be getting used to the way a new fashion looks. The pointed toe hasn't been around too long—it may seem long and ungainly to you if you've been wearing round toes for years. Wait for the world to catch up with Fashion. A year from now you may be giving away your round-toed shoes, feeling dowdy if you aren't wearing points.

Evening shoes:

The easy formula is to match the color of your dress. But again there are no rules. Heels need not be high. I have worn thong sandals to a country-club dance. Shoes can be barefoot bare, the way many of our best-designed sandals are today. Or they may be completely covered, because the classical pump is always here to stay. Jeweled heels can be very interesting. Brocades or prints can make a costume.

BAGS, SCARVES, HATS, GLOVES

Bags as Fashion . . . and to serve your needs:

One big bag, of course; but are you asking too much of it? Just because it *is* big it will hold everything, but sometimes you don't *need* everything. There have been far too many cartoons about what a woman's handbag contains! And don't forget there comes a time when you must transfer to another bag, a smaller later-day kind of bag. Big leather carryalls are not for cocktail parties or dinner dates.

Your most-of-the-time bag should be good leather, not plastic. Real for what it is, always. Alligator if you can afford it—never simulated. I find my light tawny leather bags go along with practically everything I wear, but black is probably the safest all-round color. I like fur bags for fall and winter, and they endure, like all good fur does if it is properly cared for. Muffs that act like bags are special and nice if you can get out your taxi money in ladylike time. Basket bags in summer seem to be an enduring fashion because they have proved practical and don't get dirty. Plastic that you can see through seems to me a little like a peek into your bureau drawers. Evening bags, like jewelry, are a matter for you. Pure gold (an oversize compact), or a beaded bag from Paris, petit point from Vienna, black satin, sequins, velvet, damask wonderfully elegant with a jeweled top.

Scarves are up to you:

Fashion hedges about scarves, shows them as incidentals, doesn't ever tell you quite what to do with them. Yet scarves grow more and more beautiful. What you *do* with a scarf is, however, much more important than the scarf itself. Beauty on its own is all very well, wonderful to look at on a counter, in the box—but look at a mess of scarves in your bureau drawer, try wearing one tied badly—and you'll wish you'd never been presented with it. I like scarves that are not too large, to wind rather high, to pin with a pin that shows or to hold down with beads and an invisible pin. I often attach the scarf to the dress to make some sort of tying a must—either loose bandanna style, or worn like a shawl, or caught with a pin, or wound in a neckband. Like the sash, the scarf can be the added color, the color in a different fabric, or an unexpected contrast in relation to the main color of the dress or suit. The designers of today's scarves are artists and perfectionists. You'll find endless patterns and colors, always in fabrics that tie well. But what are you going to *do* with the scarf after you've brought it home? I think the problem of the scarf arises because you expect too much of it. After all, it *can't* tie itself!

Your head:

Once upon a time you had to wear a hat. You don't *have* to today. But suddenly you may realize that your hair can't live up to all kinds of wind and weather. A hat should really be a hat. Ladylike. With great dignity and charm and distinction. For the woman who knows how to wear one, mak-

ing eyes more important, with hair sleek and neat underneath, it's a new experience, one that you may enjoy.

Glove compartment:

A woman without gloves is a marked woman. It's like going barefoot to be without them. Gloves are traditionally a sign of dignity. They should never be conspicuous, never trimmed, only well-fitted, with tapering fingers. Never wear jewelry outside of gloves. Try to blend gloves with your clothes or choose white or skin tones. Don't try to match; no two fabrics dye alike; and don't have gloves made from the same fabric as your suit—you will be disappointed. Kid or pigskin will look much smarter.

Everyone needs a good glove collection: short, long, glacé, doeskin, pigskin, cotton. Short gloves suit some people, some clothes and some occasions very well, but longer ones, crushed at the wrist, are more dignified.

I am sure I will find at least three or four pairs of white cotton gloves in your collection. Women seem, contrarily, to be much more aware of gloves in the summertime than they are the rest of the year when a pair of much used black suedes will "do" for all day and all occasions. Perhaps it is because bare arms seem conspicuous in the city and a spanking clean pair of white gloves is a dressed-up touch. Blessed be the bare arms—they made you glove-conscious. But think of the rest of the year. Have you a single pair of light gloves—white or beige—for late-day occasions, to do miracles for you if you go on to the theater after dinner? Gloves, like earrings, have a way of losing their mates, but the price of good gloves is not too high to limit you to too few. Glove manufacturing, like scarf designing, has reached a stage of perfection. Even the finest kid is washable. Cleaning bills are no longer an excuse. And Grandma's words of wisdom, "A lady is known by her shoes and her gloves," still holds.

Glove etiquette:

I don't think the twentieth century calls for a chart on gloves. Modern living doesn't make eight-button, twelve-button rules—common sense and Fashion acknowledge this. Longer than short will take you through most formal occasions. But when to take gloves *off* may pose a few problems. When you go to a cocktail party, even if your satin or velvet gloves are an integral part of your costume, *don't* touch the hors d'oeuvre tray until you have removed your gloves. And *try*, though this is merely aesthetic, to replace your right-hand glove after you've removed it to scrabble for taxi fare, because you will look much nicer entering the restaurant with both gloves on!! (The exclamations mean it so seldom happens.)

The small things, as you see, become pretty major when you list them. Each is important in itself. Searching for it, finding it, will give you a sense of accomplishment and pleasure. This part of your collection demands constant attention. Everything must be in perfect working order—clasps must clasp, on necklaces and on bags and on belts. Soap and water and the cleaner must hover like guardian angels. Gloves must be spotless, scarves pressed. Certain standards are necessary in fashion, just as they are necessary in all ways of living. If you slip, you slide into the one thing, perhaps, that will always defeat good Fashion, because carelessness for one moment can undo hours of careful planning. If the beige gloves you chose so carefully for the beige and black outfit are dirty, the whole point of the beige and black outfit will be lost. You can't substitute white ones, or pink ones, or gray ones. The costume is only a costume when the beige gloves are worn with it.

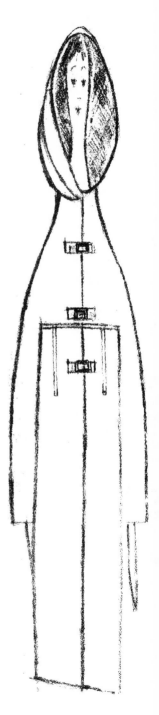

CHAPTER 4

DON'T BUY A BASIC COAT—COLLECT

D ON'T MAKE COATS too basic. This remark may startle
you—you have heard the opposite so many times. I can't
agree with the "one really good coat" because I think you will
get tired of it long before you have had your money's worth
out of it. A warm coat—a real coat—is hanging in your closet
or covering your back at least six months out of the year. If it
is a sensible color—black, brown, beige, gray—it will do a
useful job for you; but how much fun are you going to get out
of it if you have to wear it day after day? If it's a shock color—
red, lavender, orange, Kelly green—how tired of it are you
going to get? If it's big and enveloping, aren't there going to
be some days when you'd like to look like a reed? If it's a reed,
aren't there certain wide-skirted dresses in your wardrobe
that simply won't go under it without distorting its shape?
By now, you will see why I believe in a collection of coats:
long ones, short ones, coats that are capes, warm ones, not-
so-warm ones, and made out of a number of things. Wool, of
course. But also suede and silk. Textured fabrics, menswear
fabrics, knitted fabrics. And velvet and corduroy and satin
and fur. This may sound like a very expensive proposition. It
won't be if you follow my plan.

Knowing that with *more* coats, no *one* coat is going to
have to take a day-after-day wearing, you don't need to spend
a princely sum on any *one* coat. Of course, you'd like a lush
tweed, woven by the best mill, from the finest yarns. But
there *are* lesser tweeds, quite as effective. Find one you like.
It may not wear as well as the lifetime tweed, imported, made

on luxury lines, but it will stay in your wardrobe a long time because you don't intend to wear it day after day or day in and day out. My plan calls for another coat . . . and still another—each spelling the other—each offering you a pleasant change—each a fashion that can live in your wardrobe for many years.

By watching sales, by planning to add at least one coat a year to your collection, you will soon find you have a pleasant choice of coats when you confront the day, the weather, the occasion. Rather than that one very expensive purchase, allocate your budget over a period of years to include the additional coats that are exactly right for the different seasons, the different occasions that will recur year after year. I can promise you that a variety of "coverings"—and that includes jackets and stoles and sweaters and capes—will do wonders for your morale as well as your Fashion reputation. One ingredient of good Fashion is certainly freshness and variety. And I am certain this quality of pleasant change depends far more on ingenuity than your pocketbook.

Let's go back to my peasant cape, bought such a long time ago. It has played so many parts, I can almost use it for a memory book. I keep it for "a change." It is a sometime, not an all-time thing.

Think of the variety of coat fashions to choose from. Polo coat. Trench coat. Coats belted in back or with tie belts. Man-tailored coats with a Chesterfield look, a velvet collar, sometimes double-breasted, sometimes with a single row of buttons. Coats that are tent-shaped or sheath-shapes or with lines like a cocoon. And what a difference in necklines. Shawl, uncollared, a V for scarves and jewels, Peter Pan, lapels. Coats with dressmaker touches, stitching meant to show, softer lines, pockets a part of the design. And think of occasion coats: for evening, for rain, for travel, for the country. And coats to go *with* things—my favorite piece-wardrobe idea. Can you honestly continue to think in terms of a major extravagance? One wonderful coat no matter what it costs cannot possibly cover all the situations you are going to encounter in a year of coat weather. Think of coats as a year-after-year investment and I'm sure you will find real excitement and satisfaction in collecting them.

Collect them at sales. The coat marked down in January is often a real collector's item. Remember the girl who found the Lanvin original on a sales rack, to stay in her wardrobe forever, even if she has to have it copied. Because piece-wardrobes are almost always sold separately, you may find one wonderful little bolero or the perfect cardigan to blend with your wardrobe.

I like the short-coat idea. Jackets can be adapted to the weather—made warmer by what you wear under them or by investing in a fur lining. And think about linings. You don't, as a rule, check your coat, so the lining is often a background frame as you sit in a restaurant with your coat thrown back or draped around your shoulders. I like patterned linings, sometimes matching the blouse you are wearing, but not necessarily. If you are afraid of pattern, at least try color. Fur seems to me to be more interesting, more luxurious, when it's worn *not to show*—just to be glimpsed.

The waiter in a restaurant in Paris chased me to the door to tell me I was wearing my coat inside-out. The black fox was on the inside; outside was discreet broadcloth. I thanked him. I couldn't really explain that I wasn't feeling like black fox that day.

Your own life will influence your daytime coat wardrobe quite specifically—what is appropriate for your kind of work, how much of the time you will spend outdoors, the kind of restaurants you choose for luncheon dates, how you commute. Your own type, your own taste will influence the fabrics you choose and the colors. Your choice is limitless. Fashion never stands still. Tweed is no longer synonymous with country and satin often goes out in the rain.

And remember that a first appearance often comes when you are wearing a coat. When you are interviewed for a job, you keep your coat on. Your future employer's first impression of you may be based on the coat you're wearing.

When you walk down the aisle of a theater, you are wearing a coat. The lights will be out when you take off your wrap; your audience has already judged you and the most beautiful dress in the world cannot alter that first impression. Coats ride buses and subways and taxicabs. Often very important rides where you want to be looking your best. A coat is not something to be dismissed lightly. What kind of company will it keep when it is tossed on the hostess's bed? Labels in coats show. This in itself should prove to you that coats are revealing, a clue to your taste and your knowledge of Fashion. But don't feel because you have an expensive label that you've achieved true Fashion success. My black peasant cape hasn't a sign of a label and I consider it one of the most fashionable items in my closet.

Fur worn for Fashion and for fun — not to be impressive.

This is the way I feel about fur. You may not agree with me, and I don't want to take away the pleasure of the mink you've been waiting for now that the children are through college. Or the sable . . . or chinchilla. If you're diamond-minded, stick to your guns. If you're mink-minded, be adamant. Because you'll never be happy in lynx.

If you like your furs to say prestige, to set a social standard, wait until you can afford the mink or the sable. Far better to be chic in black broadcloth than to feel frustrated in a lesser fur. But if you like your furs to spell Fashion, you can have a lot of fun.

I like my furs to peek out as linings or to look kind of moth-eaten and raggedy or to be quite bold. Perhaps the simplest way to illustrate is to open the cedar closet.

The first thing I see is a black fox bundle, as bulky as a bear. But it doesn't always have to look like a bear. A turn-about makes it a serious-minded coat of fine black broadcloth lined with fur. Because fox is soft, you can pull the coat close to you, be as warm as a fur coat can make you feel, but not look as bulky as a fur coat can make you look. There's a black fox hat, too—shaped like a flower-pot, the fur fringing the forehead like a silky bang. Used as fur by itself; never to wear with the black fox coat.

Next, asking for attention, is the jaguar with bolder spotting than leopard. My colors are usually tawny, and the black, attention-getting spots are good accents. This is a three-quarter coat, with man-tailored notched lapels. It's a fine windbreaker but not too cozy so I often fill the V-neck with a long tail of soft brownish fur that is probably some kind of otter. I saw it at my furriers and forgot to ask *what* fur. It didn't really matter because it was soft and I knew it would feel wonderfully warm. Off, it looks somewhat bedraggled and weary, but wearing it I think of it as looking glamorous because it *feels* glamorous.

You've seen vicuña woven in the most sumptuous kind of polo cloth in the world. My vicuña is just hairs, the way they come before they're woven. It's a wild wonderful tawny coat that doesn't really have the nerve to call itself fur. But it's Fashion. I like it because it's always in motion—a little like a motley-colored wig until you put it on. Then, somehow it becomes modern, surrealist-modern.

You'll find nutria and moleskin in my closet, as I think you would expect to. These are mouse-colored understated furs but don't underestimate them. Understatement, like underselling, can be effective and positive. I have a piece of moleskin as long as a scarf but it's sewed to make a circle. I put this on over my head and cuddle into it. It's not a scarf and not a stole and not a cape but it keeps me warm and most people think it's something new in collars. But I'll admit you can get trapped in it—especially with waiters.

Mink? Yes, I have it on a small scale. It's a scarf now, lined with black broadcloth. I have never worn it mink-side out and never expect to—but it's a very handsome background piece. It didn't work for me at all as the cape it was originally.

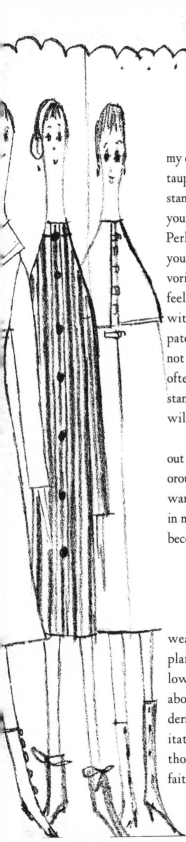

Basic colors — if not basic coats.

Looking again at my own clothes closet, I find that all my coats follow my favorite basic colors: black, brown, beige, taupe, gray. This may be a good tip for you to follow. For instance, in raincoats. Just because it's a dull day when you wear your raincoat, don't think you have to come out in bright red. Perhaps bright red will clash with everything about you, your own coloring, the clothes the raincoat covers. My favorite raincoat is black, some kind of water-proofed wool that feels confortable in raw weather, cut on trench-coat lines, with black patent leather for fastening detail. I wear black patent leather boots with it. But warmer rainy weather may not seem to go with somber colors. In my resort collections I often make raincoats really bright. Roman stripes, for instance—wide brilliant ones—and a matching skirt so nothing will clash when the raincoat is unfastened.

I like hooded coats, to keep the rain off, cold out, to peer out from as ingenuously as Little Red Riding Hood or as glamorously as Greta Garbo. Hoods can be pushed back, pulled forward; they frame your face and give my favorite effect of clothes in motion. They are graceful even when they are not hooding, become a soft cowl-shaped collar which is very flattering.

Weather-proof wizardry.

Because of whatever they do to rainproof fabrics, you can wear satin-twill, corduroy, sateen, cotton, even velvet in plain colors or printed designs. You may like traditional yellow oilcloth, sou'wester style, or very thin rubber. I hesitate about transparent plastics because what you're wearing underneath may look awfully silly in the rain. And without hesitation, I beg you to forget the space-literature ugliness of those plastic rubbers that try to look like boots. I *must* be faithful in my own fashion to Fashion, and I cannot see the logic of making my feet look ugly even if it's a way to keep them dry.

Umbrellas.

Man-size, not small and sissy. The black silk wrapped tight to look like a cane is best. Gold and pearl handle, or the natural color of wood. Top is black, beige, gray, or striped or plaid for the right occasion.

Summer cover-ups.

Even if it's 90 degrees in the shade, I doubt if you want to venture out to a restaurant lunch looking too bare. Sometimes jewelry can compensate for a bare look. Sometimes a scarf. Stoles can be gossamer thin, and you may even welcome a heavier silk for an air-cooled restaurant. I still feel little jackets are going to get quite a lot of mileage, summer after summer. Bright or unobtrusive, your summer wardrobe will tell you which. My favorite is the thinnest silk imaginable in an unrememberable color, beige perhaps, or just pale. It has a rubber band at the waist in back to give it a casual Eisenhower-jacket look. The collar is squared, like a middy collar. The sleeves are three-quarters so all your bracelets will show and your wrists will stay cool. It seems to blend just as well with gray linen as with linen in beige and brown tones. And it makes me feel dressed up enough for the most elegant restaurant.

Because linen still looks like linen but no longer wrinkles like linen, jackets made of this serviceable, washable, nicely cool fabric are good buys. Short ones, bolero type, vest type with tiny sleeves, loose unbuttoned mandarin style, or buttoned cardigans are attractive tops for a black linen sleeveless dress.

Fashion likes sweaters, dresses them up with ribbons and jewels and embroidery, or lets the cashmere speak its own elegance. I think perhaps sweaters have ended fancy summer evening coats. But just as I make a statement like that I realize that long summer coats in matching or contrasting colors are really a wonderful idea.

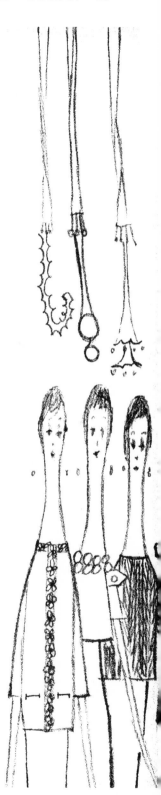

Decide on your own summer cover-up. The piece-wardrobe idea is especially good in summer, because you can add or subtract according to the thermometer. Skirt, sleeveless vest or blouse with more sleeve. Very short bolero jacket or a longer jacket or coat, depending on noon or night. One beautifully co-ordinated outfit may see you through all the important occasions the summer offers.

You can be imaginative with summer cover-ups, because summer is a fancy-free kind of season. If you like scarves and have a way with tying them, look for beautiful prints or striking colors. The stole has been knitted in every conceivable way, as a lacy-knit, or like a piece of homespun, the way the Mexicans and Guatemalans do it. I know a woman who made a bolero out of a white candlewick bedspread—the snowflake look was amusing., the cotton was cool. I know another who wore a pale gray chiffon coat made like a kimono to her city job, looking wonderfully airy and cool on the hottest days, yet she was completely covered. You are not limited to cottons, linens, silks. Very lightweight wool jersey, the thinnest challis, is actually no hotter than the materials you think of as being cool.

Don't overlook the marketplace on your summer tour. Summertime is vacation time for most of us. When you cross a border, go to the marketplace, look for native shawls, scarves, head-coverings. You may find, as I did, the lifetime sash, the pink one woven in heavy cotton thread by a Basque peasant. Remember the matador's black velvet jacket, to top a white lace evening dress. Remember the Mexican bolero, sometimes sleeveless, with its bold scrolls of gold braid. Remember the Clan plaid scarf. Marabou was once for bedrooms. I know someone who dares to wear it for summer evenings.

Evening coats.

I like them long because I think that long dresses and long coats are universally becoming. You may not like my own collection of evening coats. Perhaps I won't like yours. It doesn't matter. Evening coats, like your jewelry and furs, are reflections of your own taste—how you like to look— not usually of what you have spent. They can be as highly individual as your evening bags. They can be you in another mood, not the one people expect of you. Even your husband, who likes to think he knows you, doesn't mind being surprised at a party.

My evening coats, or cloaks, are so un-eveningish I am almost afraid to describe them. Perhaps the word cloaks is the clue. I think that women should practice a little mystery after nightfall. I like to be really cloaked— from head to toe. My rule is, if it's long, let it be really long. You are going to blink when I tell you what my cloaks are made of. One is the familiar daytime polo-coat material in conventional pale beige. It is cut like a polo coat, goes straight down to the floor and is worn without a belt or sash. The lining, a beautiful lavender and white taffeta print, matches the dress I wear with the coat. Together, they make a costume. Another is gray flannel. Then there is the dark green tweed cut like a child's nightgown, with a wide quaint cape collar. The coat is lined with ivory satin twill. I might wear the black peasant cape on a really stormy night. It is as dramatic as the Count of Monte Cristo and the inside pockets are fine for holding things like glasses that won't fit into my evening bag. My calico evening cloak is fine for summer fun. I copied it word for word from a museum piece. It is made in layers and I wear it, looking bulky on purpose and feeling as gay as if I were off to a husking bee.

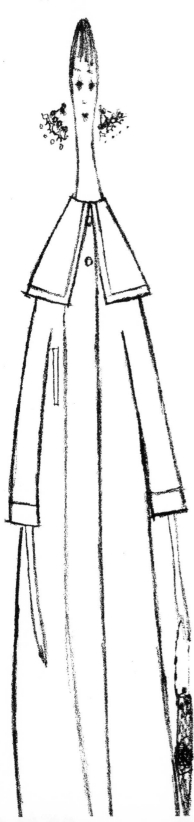

Costume look.

Checking the kind of evening coats I have described, you will see that I have tried for a costume look. Festive occasions are historical in their way; lean a little on the past, relax a little from this year's trend. Charity balls often choose a costume theme—fans, headdresses or period pieces. The Mardi Gras is famous for its beautiful masked and mysterious ladies. Don't we almost expect a costumed look at a big gala affair?

I want to be covered to my toes like a puritan. You may feel happier in a ballet-length dress or short sheath and Dame Fashion will accept your choice—seem to be saying "Use your imagination, wear whatever you please as long as it is beautiful and makes you feel beautiful."

Yet, even if it defies Dame Fashion, let me tell you what I feel. *Never* miss an opportunity to wear a long dress—most becoming to everyone; and why women gave them up for short things, I'll never understand. Every woman, no matter what her size or shape, has a chance to look more attractive in a long dress. Each of us will choose the fabric we like best. You may feel silly in a wool jersey evening dress, a polo coat acting like an evening coat. Evening is your own affair and Fashion gives you complete freedom. I might like gold cloth cut like a string bean; you might like it looking harem.

Coats plus.

When you have gathered a real collection, you can take another step and get a coat and a dress that go together—never to be separated, never to be worn with any other dress or any other coat, and always with a special feeling of satisfaction. If you take a little trouble, you may be able to manage a heavy fabric skirt to go with the coat. If you are lucky you may find an odd skirt that blends with the tweed or plaid for a welcome "extra." The store can probably get an extra length of material from the manufacturer. Blending shirts or sweaters with a color in the tweed is another way to make your coat a wardrobe. If you buy an extravagantly gay and beautiful coat remember to wear it over a simple dress. Don't wear everything at once—it's a great American fault.

More than one basic coat in your life. Try it. Coats should be there to play around with. Even if months go by without useful duty on the part of all of them, there will be that one occasion where "another coat" fits exactly. And using my plan of adding and keeping, there will be more and more "other coats" as the system starts working.

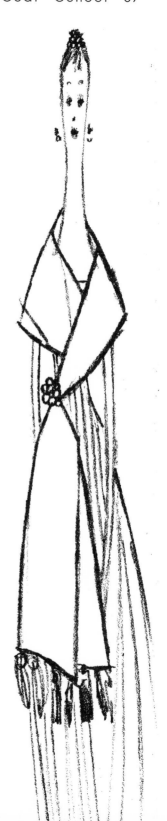

CHAPTER 5

LET MRS. JONES
KEEP UP WITH YOU

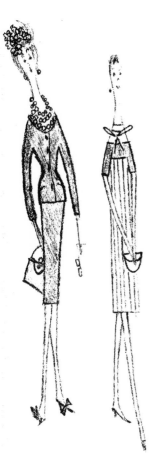

B Y NOW YOU KNOW I don't believe the amount of money decides the amount of Fashion. If you are intelligent about clothes, there will be no question of trying to live up to Mrs. Jones. Before you know it, Mrs. Jones will be trying to live up to you. She may do a double-take when she sees the red shoelace tied around your neck, but she will probably begin to wonder if she has been relying too long on her pearls. Mrs. Jones may have expensive labels in her clothes, and the fine lines that go with expensive labels. If you are smart you will forget labels and look for fine lines. You are fortunate because you live in a country where mass-produced clothes include clothes that follow the best precepts in Fashion. Soft dress-maker touches that mean elegance, gentle shoulder lines, just as many interesting necklines to choose from in a $29.95 range as in a custom-made collection.

"Made-for-you touches" —that's really what a "dressmaker" suit is. Your waist in the right place, your shoulders relatively your own, and buttons that can be moved an eighth of an inch and still fit buttonholes. Draping where you *need* it, the hemline in exact proportion to your height, your width, and at the most flattering point. Quite truthfully, it's all easier if it's custom-made but to challenge you, it *can* be found in ready-made lines and with a few strategic alterations seem to have been designed just for you. Never for a moment forget the joy of a dress or hat or shoe "made for you"—but if custom-made is out of the ques-tion, apply the principles of custom-made to the clothes you can afford to buy. What are these principles?

First—if it's custom-made it fits perfectly. In a previous chapter I have warned you to learn not only your size but to know where alterations will be necessary. Then learn to economize on alterations. A few over-all things to remember. A shoulder alteration is always more expensive than easing a waistline. Take a size 10 in preference to a size 12, if the only problem of fit is at the waist, providing, of course, that there are enough seams to let out. Similarly, if the tightness is in the hips, check the seams. In this case, you may have to take the size 12 and cope with lifting and narrowing the shoulders.

Second—if it's custom-made it is usually a design that relies on line. It isn't covered with sewed bows, buttons that have no relation to buttoning, glitter added on, fake pockets. So, in less expensive clothes, look for simplicity and honest detail. And be afraid of "too much."

Third—if it's custom-made it avoids stiff or hard designing. Be careful of the man-tailored suit that is too tailored. *His* gray flannel can't be *yours*. There must be adaptations to your figure, your femininity—perhaps a brown velveteen collar, a change in where the pockets go. Custom-made clothes are made of fabrics that drape softly, mold, reveal. The coat-dress that sells for $14.95 will never resemble the coat-dress from a designer's workroom, because the stiff unyielding fabric that is used will make the design look just "coat." Your rule then is to avoid the inexpensive dress that is made of hard unyielding fabric. Keep on searching until you have found a dress at a price you can pay that is made of a becoming fabric. *Feel* the material—is it soft, a pleasant surface to touch?

Your taste can be as sound as anyone's if you are guided by sound fashion ideas. A general safeguard is to avoid extreme fashions. Yet there are exceptions. I told you in the last chapter that big evenings invite adventure in Fashion. And you can be less conservative when you are in a leisurely setting: pants and a bold shirt to entertain informally; vivid colors for vacation landscapes or to follow a sport. Still, your major rule should be "conservative." For a daytime wardrobe, extreme fashions will highlight too much. You are in the

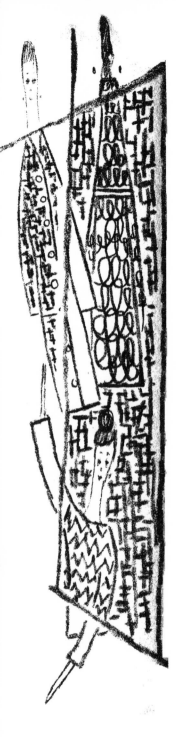

public eye, even if it's only on a shopping tour. You don't want heads to turn. You don't want to be misunderstood.

When you go shopping, don't go with too many preconceived ideas of what you are going to look for. (A red dress because every fashion magazine is showing one. A tunic because Mrs. Jones looks so elegant in hers.) If your mind is a squirrel-cage jammed with impressions you've picked up here and there, you are apt to come away with a headache and a bad purchase. Your first question to yourself should be: "Is it becoming?" To know what is becoming, you must know your own figure. If your hips are large, forget the tight skirt, even though you long for it. The idea is to train yourself not to long for something that can't be becoming because it is all wrong for your figure. You will never feel at ease in it. Your wide hips may be compensated for by a small waist. Make the most of it. A wide skirt will make it look even smaller.

Assembling an on-the-job, in-the-public-eye daytime wardrobe takes great discipline. How to be conservative—and not dull? How to hint—and not shout?

Universal daytime fabrics.

Certain fabrics, certain textures, convey a feeling of time and place. You feel comfortable and well-dressed wearing them in broad daylight. You should know them all, choose those that make the best clothes for you. You may have to rule out certain ones for personal reasons. "If it's too tweedy, I itch." "Jersey is too clingy for my figure." "Cotton has to be pressed too often." "I hate girdles—so knitted clothes are not for me."

Find, then, the fabrics that are appropriate for your daytime life and investigate their possibilities. Think of them in terms of what they will make: suits, dresses, skirts, blouses—and which of these dominate your wardrobe?

Think of them in the shapes they take: narrow lines, full or
pleated skirts, soft draping. Which will make "tops" to move
around in your wardrobe, and what fabrics will be most apt to
appear in tailored shirts, scooped blouses, turtle necklines?

Jot down the word *tweed* and see what comes to your mind.
Tweed can be bulky or very smooth, flecked or a patterned
weave. Tweed is usually color-with-color, the heather or speck-
led idea. It may be the established combinations, black-white,
black-brown, gray-white, or blends of one color in lighter and
darker shades. Tweed has elegance, even fragrance—they actually named a perfume after it. You know that you want something in tweed—but *where* are you going to wear it?

Tweed-urban means tweed shaped slim, in a skirt with
either a long coat to match or a traditional suit jacket. If the
skirt is wider, the top will probably be a bolero or a stole.
And if the tweed is light in weight, you may find it makes a
useful warm dress for winter weather, but remember it is
warm and may prove uncomfortable in a heated office.

Tweed-country, its natural media, may be a big warm enveloping coat or a jacket or series of jackets to wear with odd
skirts or a suit that will carry you all through autumn and
even into a sunny December day. A three-piece tweed, with
both short *and* full-length coat, may prove the best investment
you've ever made.

Tweed-travel is absolutely at home on trains and ships and
planes and almost anywhere in the world except the tropics.

Tweed-evening occurs in my wardrobe—I've described
the green tweed full-length evening cloak lined with satin-
twill. Perhaps just for me.

You can see what a really universal fabric it is. In pastels,
it goes to resorts and country clubs. You find it in stoles and
pants and shorts. It is a tradition in England. You will always
feel well-dressed wearing it.

There are other universal fabrics, each with its reputation
for elegance and good taste. Wool jersey, cotton, linen, satin-
twill, and of course the miracle fabrics that stretch and stay
put, that dry in a minute, that refuse to wrinkle. What your

daytime clothes are made *of* should be one of the first consid-erations when you shop.

What about fabrics for traditional occasions—satin, lace, organdy, velvet, for big evenings and weddings and debuts and graduations? These are more difficult fabrics to decide upon because they are only beautiful when they are woven from the finest threads, and *when* they are, of course, far more fragile than the daytime fabrics we have been talking about.

Satin and lace and organdy can be avoided. In my life they are. They have been imitated and cheapened to a point where they no longer necessarily stand for great elegance. However, if you can afford silk-backed Lyons velvet (a cotton velveteen can never have the sheen of silk-velvet), if you can afford hand-made lace, and if you a cope what what goes *under* organdy (because whatever it is will show)—by all means indulge in these luxury fabrics.

I have found that wool jersey is every bit as regal as vel-vet; white chiffon will out-float satin any time, and an em-bossed cotton can have far more beauty and richness than a flimsy piece of machine-made lace.

If you are farsighted, you will think about having a wed-ding dress, a graduation dress, a dress for your daughter's debut, made for more than one great occasion. Try having it made in pieces. Keep it simple in cut, in a good fabric, and have a black top made to wear with the skirt later. It can be the basis for many evening occasions. The top may be perfect with a long bright skirt; the white or pastel skirt may con-trast boldly with a simple dark top. A long white piqué for graduation can be chopped off short and the sleeves taken out fir a very useful summer sheath.

Surprise combinations in fabrics.

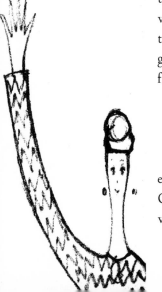

My polo coat, cut to the floor and used for evenings, is an example. Remember it is combined with a silk taffeta lining. One very high-fashion designer likes to blend gray flannel with white satin. You can do the same. There are white satin blouses to buy, and satin by the yard to line your jacket. The little fur collars on sweaters and wool dresses act like fabric, not like fur. Combine suede with what your own knitting needles make, far more interesting than an all-knit dress. An imaginative use of surprise combinations is emphatically good Fashion, and Mrs. Jones will wonder why she didn't think of it.

When to buy.

There are many Fashion calendars. The Seventh Avenue calender may help you. We show the buyers our fall and winter clothes in May and June. They put in their orders. The clothes will not appear in the stores until August. And no matter what the thermometer says, if you want the *first* of the new autumn things, you had better look for them in August. If you wait until the first cold day in October to buy, the best clothes may be gone, at least in the average sizes. It is true that the stores will reorder, but the coat you liked in a certain fabric may come back in another fabric. The mills may have stopped making that particular pattern, so another has had to be substituted. In late autumn, when you are busy wearing your new fall clothes, the designers are busy working on resort clothes and early spring clothes. Again the buyers come and look and choose, and in late December and January the clothes make their appearance in the stores. Unless your routine does an unpredictable lot of jumping around, you must know what you will need next summer. The resort collections are the best head-start I can think of. The ten dollars extra you may pay for a cotton in January can mean ten dollars' worth of extra pleasure next summer. You will own the dress, and be ready to wear it *before* the standard summer stock is in the store. Resort clothes have a little more flair, are often made from limited patterns, so you are not as apt to see as many duplicates. You need not worry about lines changing. Summer collections follow the general trend of resort and spring collections.

The fashion magazines and the fashion reporters for every

newspaper in the country are in league with you. As early as December 1, they are showing you the bathing suits they like, the color combinations they feel are here to stay. And their tips are sound. They have been *educated*, for years, to appraise and to predict. And they know that Fashion likes changes, and they are eager to spot them. One year it may be the *maillot*, a one-piece bathing suit cut on simple figure-fitting lines. If they tell you about it, you may be very sure there will be many one-piece bathing suits worn by the best-dressed women in America. You will know in January whether sheaths are holding their own, whether fuller skirts or pleats are going to give them a run for their money. Don't confuse the editorial pages of a magazine with the advertising pages. The advertising pages are clearly marked with the label or name of the manufacturer. What is shown on those pages is what the manufacturer has to offer. He has done his best to appraise and predict, but he is not always a Fashion authority. The editorial pages have sifted and chosen the best, the newest news, to report to you, and the whole weight of Fashion knowledge and Fashion authority lies behind the clothes that are shown editorially.

If you can make a Singer sing, perhaps you can catch onto a whole new idea in January and spend the winter months remaking your wardrobe. And because winter resort clothes often borrow from the woolen family, (lightweight jersey, challis, sweater tops) there may be a *find* in January that can walk right out under your winter coat. I can think of an example right now. In my current resort collection, there is a three-piece outfit: olive-green wool jersey skirt, brilliant turquoise wool jersey blouse, olive-green wool jersey jacket. The jersey is literally weighed in ounces so there is nothing bulky about it. The colors are sufficiently subdued to blend with winter weather. And the whole thing can be an early-spring tonic—the lift in the wardrobe that has been serving you since fall. The long leisurely terrace or cabaña dress in the resort collection may be the perfect answer to evenings at home in a warm apartment. You may not be able to go to

Florida, but you can have Florida fun, and your January investment will serve you well into summer. Chop off the skirt of the long cotton when you're tired of it for evenings at home. It will be just as successful as a short summer dress.

Be an early bird.

Buy at least one major item *before* the season gets under way. Pick up the rest of your seasonal wardrobe at the normal buying period.

Learn to watch for sales.

Perhaps you are vague about the time of year you can count on sales. You can expect merchandise to be reduced when the height of the season is over. You can always count on clearance after holidays: Easter, Fourth of July, Christmas. Announcements will be made in the newspapers, but if you are smart you will try to get in on the bargains before the general public reads about them. Mot stores hold private sales before announcing a clearance to the public. Charge-account customers receive invitations several days ahead of the newspaper ad. But you don't need to have an invitation or to be a charge-account customer to attend a private sale. So keep an eye on the stores prior to the time you might expect a sale.

Beware of "padded" sales—merchandise that is cheap but looks too new, brought in to swell the racks. Look for the dress that has been around if it has a label you can trust. Never mind the torn thread, the tiny tear. If the label is one you associate with good quality, you can be sure that the dress is made of good fabric and that the workmanship lives up to the name of the designer. The small tear will not affect the lifetime of the dress. The dress may be soiled but it can be cleaned. A belt may be missing, but belts may be substituted. The good lines are still there and the label tells you that the integrity of a name designer is represented in the dress. You can trust the sales advertised by big-name stores just as you can trust the clothes

with name labels. There are often second markdowns but it is always a gamble to wait if you have found a real bargain. There are more women than you'd suspect who know that the dress with a good label, no matter how shopworn, is the real buy. High fashions sometimes stay on the rack longer because many women are afraid of a radical change in silhouette. But remember, the fashion that looks too new today may be the one everyone will be wearing a year from now.

How you choose your clothes in the first place will affect the lifetime of your wardrobe. A suit should be *your* suit—not a spring suit or a fall suit. If you buy it in the spring, you'll also wear it in the early fall; if you buy it in the fall, you'll wear it again in the spring. The difference will be in what you wear under it. In the fall, perhaps with a sweater; in the spring with a fresh white blouse. A fur or stole can be added for an extra layer of warmth.

Follow a color pattern.

Get things that go together. When you find a dressmaker suit you may also have acquired the perfect jacket for some of your summer cottons, providing you have given a second thought to the colors that predominate in your wardrobe.

Mrs. Jones firmly believes that money will make her well-dressed. But if Mrs. Jones goes wrong on line or color, everything cancels out. No dress, even if it is a $1000 import from a Paris *couturier*, can stand alone. It needs a wearer—the right wearer. It needs to be worn for the right occasion. And it needs the right accessories. No dress can stand on its own.

The fundamentals then are not dollars and cents. They are how you buy, how you distribute your Fashion budget, and the relation of the clothes to yourself and your life. Everything in Fashion has been done before—but it is always different as it is worn by you.

CHAPTER 6

IS IT THE FAULT OF
THE DRESS?

TOO OFTEN WHEN you've made a bad buy, you put the blame on the dress. I think the mistake usually begins in the fitting room when for any number of reasons you say "Yes" too quickly, or an unconsidered "No."

Often, to see with my own eyes just what happens to the clothes I have designed, I have followed them to the stores and enlisted myself as a saleswoman. What, for instance, makes one model a sell-out and another a poor thing destined for some future sales rack? Sometimes the answers are easy. "Colors too daring for the average taste." "Asks for the perfect figure." But I am certain there are other things, quite incidental things, that may send you away from the store with the wrong dress—or with the frustration of no dress at all.

Consider underclothes.

Does it surprise you to have me reach underthings by this roundabout route? It wouldn't if you had followed me into the fitting room. "But my brassiere straps show!" the lady says with a faint note of outrage in her voice. The brassiere she is wearing probably cost three dollars, the dress at least ten times as much— the dress she *liked* until the brassiere straps showed. Yet, without anything more than a quick flash of irritation, she discards the dress and never considers the possibility of wearing a different kind of brassiere. This seems to me to be one of those blind gestures, out of habit, in line with proverbial human behavior. Don't put the cart before the horse. But how many of us do it.

My favorite dinner dress is a navy-blue Empire dress with a scoop neck that must lie flat to look right. I found that by slitting the back a good ten inches, catching it at the nape with a tiny button, the front of the dress looked wonderful. Naturally I can't let a brassiere fitting show through the important slit in the back. But do *all* brassieres fasten just below the shoulder blades? I think of the many satisfying times I have worn the blue dinner dress. Wouldn't it have been silly to give it up because I couldn't cope with a brassiere?

Don't wear too much underneath your clothes. A half-slip is better than a full slip in many cases. With brassiere straps and slip straps, too, you have four shoulder straps to manage. Lined dresses, eliminating slips, are wonderful in the summer. The old-fashioned camisole, combining slip and panty, is beginning to be new-fashioned. Most girdles have lost their bones but still do a good architectural job. If you are really slender, you may go without a girdle; nobody minds a slightly rounded look if your posture is disciplined. Don't think that because you are wearing a girdle, you can slump. And try on a girdle before you buy it—all kinds aren't for you.

Scenery makes a difference.

The most glamorous dress in the world loses much of its glamour if it is worn on a bare stage. The fitting room is bare and often it is hard to imagine a bathing suit on a beach when you are seeing it in a cubby-hole. With a great expanse of sand and sea around me, I felt overdressed in the bathing suit that had seemed to me almost too brief when I tried it on. Try to imagine scene and setting when you try on a ball gown. Think of it under soft lights rather than the harsh daylight of the fitting room.

Saleslady's tactics.

"It looks just like you," she says sweetly and you don't believe a word of it. Temperamentally irritated by the sales-

*Claire McCardell's Monastic
dress, an unfitted shift dress with a
self-tie waist, was launched in 1938
to smashing success. Exclusively
manufactured by Best & Co. as
the "Nada" dress, it put McCardell
on the map thanks to its popular,
innovative design, which allowed
the wearer to tie it however she chose.*

*Originally created in blue denim
in 1942, the Pop-over dress featured
a built-in apron, large pockets,
and even an attached oven mitt.
It became an American fashion
staple, available in a variety of
fabrics, and McCardell was
awarded a citation of honor for
the design by the American Fashion
Critics' Award.*

Model Sabine (left) wears Claire McCardell's Pantung Loincloth swimsuit, and Janet Stevenson models the Hug Me Tights suit designed by McCardell's Parsons classmate Joset Walker. The way these suits showed off the female body was considered shocking for the day.   1946. © Genevieve Naylor/CORBIS

Models pose in summer dresses by Claire McCardell.
1946. © Genevieve Naylor/CORBIS

Claire McCardell's "sunburn-brown jersey beachwear," featured in a Kaiser and Frazer automobile advertisement in 1948. The ad quotes McCardell likening her glamorous yet useful clothing to the functional car: "The beauty of these original designs is based on utility. No wonder women fall in love with them."

A signature Claire McCardell for Townley dress in "Stone-cutter tissue faille," featured in an ad for Enka Rayon yarn circa 1951.

An "Active Sports Ensemble," ideal for vacations, designed by Claire McCardell for Townley in 1952. The model wears a silk sleeveless blouse printed with tiny checks and matching silk pedal pushers. © Bettmann/CORBIS

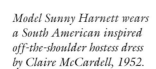

Model Sunny Harnett wears a South American inspired off-the-shoulder hostess dress by Claire McCardell, 1952.

Claire McCardell (seated at table) surrounded by models wearing her designs and accessories, including jewelry, shoes, gloves, hats, and sunglasses. 1954. © Mark Shaw/mptvimages.com

Claire McCardell sets her designing mind on the sweater, and witness her brilliant conclusions! Knitted by Canterbury, they get the fine full-fashioning they deserve. Tycora's the luxurious yarn they take shape in...it's a never-pill, never-fuzz miracle that leads a pretty soft life, yet keeps its shape, for keeps! Just two from a wonderful collection...the Bateau and the Criss-cross Turtle Neck, both in white, red, green, beige, gold, turquoise, black and navy. Sizes 34 to 40. $7.95.

"AMSCOT — NEW AMERICAN DESIGNS KNIT IN THE OLD SCOTTISH TRADITION." CANTERBURY KNITTERS, LTD., 1410 BROADWAY, NEW YORK 18, N. Y.

CANTERBURY'S Full-fashioned
Amscot collection in Tycora®
designed by
Claire McCARDELL

Two examples of Claire McCardell's classic sweater designs from 1956: the Bateau and the Criss-Cross Turtle Neck, knitted by Canterbury with "never-pill" Tycora yarn and retailing at $7.95 each.

BY CLAIRE McCARDELL

WHAT SHALL I WEAR?

The What, Where, When and How Much of Fashion

Claire McCardell clothing label in a Monastic dress.

Photo © Julie Gury, JoulesVintage, Vintage Fashion Guild member.

The original jacket of What Shall I Wear? The What, Where, When and How Much of Fashion, *first published in 1956.*

woman, perhaps tired when you make your decision, it is no wonder so many wrong judgments are made.

Look for trouble.

Remember to sit down in the dress or suit before you say, "I'll take it." The most astonishing things can happen when you try sitting down in the skirt that looked perfect when you *stood* in front of the mirror. Consider *where* the zipper is. You may live alone and like it, but you may regret it if you wrench your arm trying to zip a back zipper into place. If you do decide on the dress with a back zipper, be sure that the top has room to spare. If the strain is too great, the zipper may slip and become a glaring indiscretion. If it sticks, you are really caught. At least a zipper misbehaving on the side can be covered with your arm. I shall never forget the woman in pink satin, a little too plump, trying to look as if it hadn't happened when everyone on the dance floor could see the back zipper on her dress caught half-way.

See where buttons button.

Perhaps you're a lady chemist or your own cook and bottle-washer. Will your sleeves roll up? Obviously they can't if your cuff buttons don't really button. Remember that buttons are bulky. Right this minute I know a girl who is grieving about a high-fashion jumper that buttons from the square low neck to about three inches below her waist. The jumper is scaled wrong for her figure and those buttons below the waist are far too prominent, actually make her look as though she weighs more than the scales say. Buttons have been known to get designers into trouble. One on Seventh Avenue, for instance, who tried to imitate a gown he had seen hurriedly in Paris. The original had big buttons in back from neckline to waistline. The copy had buttons all the way down to the hem. Plainly a dress nobody could sit through a play in. And because they were sewed buttons without buttonholes, nobody could even get the dress on.

Mass production has caused shortcuts: buttons that won't button, ready-made bows sewed on. Often you can alter details in an inexpensive dress to make it live up to custom-made techniques. The inexpensive skirt with an appliquéd arrow to hold the kick-pleat is an example. How easy to rip off the appliqué and embroider an arrow or narrow bar, the kind of hand detail you will find in better skirts.

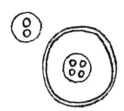

Watch how necklines fit.

Do they gape like the top of a paper bag when you are sitting any way but upright? No matter how pretty the lace on your slip may be, it's not twentieth century to show it. I like high round necks because they stay put and are a focal spot for jewelry. I think scoop necklines are feminine and flattering. A square neckline fits better if it is slightly curved at the corners, just enough to help it cling, without spoiling the square line. Don't blame the dress if the bare-top design makes some of you roll over the top. There are other ways to look bare, not so hard on your figure. A deep V. A backless dress, very effective with a covered front. Or a very open squared neckline. To save your energy and the salesgirl's time, make decisions before you go to the fitting room. You know by now what your figure can and can't wear.

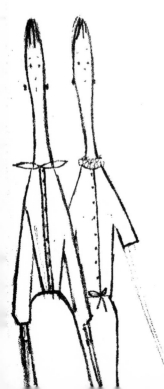

A wearable trouble-free wardrobe.

This is what I strive for when I design. My most wearable dress is probably the "Popover"—a straight shift that goes over your head, with no zipper to zip, no buttons to button, no fastenings at all. In certain stretchable fabrics, the boat-shaped neck is used. In others, there is a deep-slit neckline that can be pinned high or low. Sometimes the dress is a sheath. With more fullness, you tie a waistline with a sash. This quick something is *really* trouble-free. In more subdued colors, it can go to the office. In an awning stripe, it shops at the supermarket. The "Nightshirt Dress" looks like the classic shirtwaist, extending to a hemline. You cinch yourself in with a leather belt, wear cuff-links that blend with the buttons down the front.

A blouse wardrobe.

Variety is the thing. Surplice, halter, vest, shirt. Some blouses collarless for jewelry display. Different fabrics. Wool jersey tops, knitted T-shirts, silky shantung, men's shirtings, thin China silk, heavy lustrous satin (mine is orange, worn with a tomato-red wool suit.) Stripes, polka dots, prints. Overblouses, fitted or looking like a middy.

Can you wear a sleeveless dress?

Yes, if your arms are slender. No, if you have overdeveloped arm muscles or any sign of flabbiness. A candid-camera shot of you in a sleeveless dress may jolt you. Your eyes are not trained to watch for the side or back view of your arms.

Can you wear pleats?

Everyone can, but everyone can't wear every kind. If you are tall, you can manage the widening look of unpressed pleats, very beautiful as you walk because they swirl and move gracefully. But if you are short, this free-flowing fashion will drown you. Accordion pleats, narrow in themselves, act like a sheath, yet achieve a pleasant air of motion when you walk. Box pleats are wide, give the illusion of *more* width. Front pleats pressed down from shoulder to knee, ending in a flounce, achieve a fitted look, seem to be becoming to most figures.

Why the cardigan is a classic.

Probably because it is universally becoming. I like the cardigan to make a pattern in itself. I use double-stitching, the kind you see on denim levis, to outline the big patch pock-

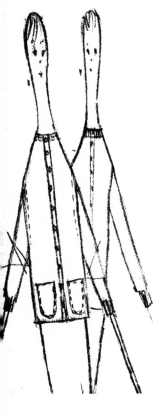

ets, trace the shoulder line and length of sleeve. I don't mean that the cardigan is made of denim. That's the fun. Once again you have a surprise combination—the stitching you'd expect on denim found on silk, cotton, flannel.

"String Bean"—and just what it says, the slender dress for slender women. Side hip pockets sometimes add shape, but pockets at the hipbone are newer. There are all kinds of things to do at the simple neckline: big beads, a chiffon scarf tied in a big bow or lots of gold chains.

Remember that certain designs are carefully calculated to call attention to certain parts of your figure. Bosom interest is not achieved merely by a dangerously low-cut neckline. Often you are completely covered to the throat but the lines of the dress are doing their subtle job of highlighting. The Empire dress with stitching or string tied under the bosom is just as siren-y as a plunging neckline. I've used striped material to make V's from waistline to neckline to accentuate the above-the-waist look. The Princess dress, completely form-fitting, uncluttered by belts, buttons, bows, can be practically Venus de Milo.

Look Magazine once said about my clothes: "Slightly sloppy to begin with, her clothes never get that wilted look." My suggestion is: check fabric first, then see how a dress works. Be wary of the dress that seems to stand by itself without anybody in it. It's anything but sloppy but it couldn't seem to stand by itself unless it had underpetticoats attached or unless it was made of a stiff fabric. Your own body isn't going to have much of a chance in this dress—it's been shaped ahead of time. It probably isn't going to be too comfortable and it will have very little to do with *your* shape.

Be aware of details.

Look for interesting necklines, the stand-up mandarin collar with ends left to tie in a quite occidental bow; cowl collars, big important cape collars. A surplice neckline is softer and easier to wear than a V. Does the sleeve feel comfortable?

If it's a continuation of the shoulder, an all-one-piece affair as opposed to the set-in sleeve, it will adjust itself to every figure. Are pockets placed right for you? If you're wide to start with, you can't afford the extra width of flaring patch pockets on both sides of a jacket. Learn to use pockets for a look of your own—pin something on them, let a colored handkerchief serve as an extra color.

This year's look.

Don't be a slave to it, but be reasonably aware of it. If it's a tent and you like to be a pole, think twice before you invest in a tent. The clothes you give away are probably the clothes that are temperamentally wrong for you. If the lines of a dress make you feel *un*like yourself, you won't be able to live with the dress. It may be too sudden—or you may adapt to parts of it slowly.

This year's newest look usually comes out of Paris. It is known in the trade as "High Fashion." High Fashion is not for everyone. Sometimes it offers a basic and beautiful idea that is easy to wear and then you can be sure it will be adapted very quickly. But often, the French idea is very special and not for our American way of life. And not everyone can afford High Fashion. The most beautiful and luxurious fabrics in the world appear in the Paris collections—satin, brocade, cloth of pure gold. "Well," I sometimes think, "you can't imitate pure gold." And this is the kind of thinking that brings me to wool jersey for an evening dress. I'd rather switch than substitute; make wool jersey a new evening fashion in its own right.

I salute Paris fashions and the years I studied in Paris gave me a knowledge of clothes that I consider priceless. But what kind of knowledge? Something far more enduring than "this year's look." What I gained, I think every woman should try to gain: a knowledgeability about clothes. The way they work, how they feel, their place in your life, the pleasure they give you. Someone once said "McCardell classic" about one

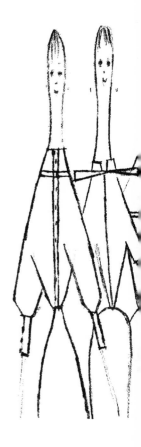

of my designs. I couldn't have had a nicer compliment. I'd much rather be a tried and true classic than *too* new. I believe that clothes should fit the individual and the occasion. They are made to be worn—to be lived in. I like comfort in the rain, in the sun; comfort for active sports, for sitting still, and for looking pretty. I do not like glitter; only fabric well-cut and beautifully constructed. The color and line of a costume should flow naturally with the body. Details should represent true feminine expression.

My own clothes stay in my wardrobe a long time. They are never made especially for me. Because I like familiar things, something that lives longer than today, I never think of clothes as being "this year's look." If you choose clothes that are basically right for you, with a hemline raised or lowered, a waistline adapted, they can be contemporary in any year.

CHAPTER 7

WHERE DO FASHION TRENDS COME FROM?

ONE WOMAN'S PERSONALITY can sometimes launch a trend. The red jersey exercise suit I did for Vera Zorina started the fad for ballerina bathing suits with tight bodices and short circular skirts. Problems arising in my life and yours ask for answers that may mean a whole new way with Fashion. Pockets solved the business of what the model does with her hands when she is swinging around the showroom. Pockets may prove equally useful to you when you are standing in front of your boss's desk trying to look casual and composed.

Outwitting tape measures often starts a trend. The wide skirt diminishes a waistline. Our less formal lives and greater leisure made casual clothes a trend. And with the world only a plane-ride apart, there has been a trend toward fashions from other countries: the Oriental look, the East Indian look.

You, too, can start a trend. For yourself. Something that can identify you, be just for you. Start with a chart of your clothes life. Put a large X beside that part of your schedule that puts you on view. Consider what role you play and your audience. How can you surprise your audience, make them pleasantly aware of you?

Suppose you're plain Jane and always look like a carbon copy of yourself. You have a wardrobe of suits, ranging from the good gray flannel to the tried-and-true glen plaid. You are wary of sweaters because they cling and don't seem right for the office. You are self-conscious in shirts. So you've settled for a series of ladylike blouses, mostly with Peter Pan collars. Sometimes you wear a plain gold bar pin at the collar. Usually

you try pearls or chains and give them up. Scarves frankly terrify you.

Obviously your new look must start with suits—you can't throw them away. First, banish the Peter Pan collars. "But they're feminine-looking—offset the masculine cut of the suits," you argue. "They're little-girl, not grown-up feminine," we answer.

"Well—*what* blouse then?" you dare us to answer?

"Perhaps no blouse," we say smiling.

Plain Jane looks shocked. But when we button her into the gray flannel with its pretty V-neckline, *her* pretty V-neckline which nobody has ever seen becomes a real point of interest. Her skin is fair and smooth. Her neck is slender. "You're going to keep that V," we say sternly, "and you're not even going to wear so much as a string of pearls to disturb the throat line. You're going to be the pin girl."

Pin by pin, Jane gave up being plain. She found big old pieces in blue glass, green glass. She found stickpins to group, jeweled pieces for lapels. She became the most feminine thing in a man-tailored suit that the office had seen for a long time. Naturally, she didn't always go without a blouse. But no more Peter Pan collars. She found V-neck waistcoats, surplice necklines, and finally she was won over to the opposite of bare—very high swan-collared jerseys that gave a sweater effect but were at home in a city office.

Of course plain Jane didn't start a trend for the rest of the world, but she did start one for herself. And who is more important than oneself?

It has been said of me that I design as I please. I wish that more women would dress as they please. How fearful some of you are: "I like sashes but a sash might make people think the dress was homemade."

Where is the X in your life? How does it affect the spending of your fashion dollars? Let's think specifically in terms of: THE TIME, THE PLACE, THE CLOTHES.

SUBURBAN A.M.

You will be in the spotlight at eight o'clock when you drive your husband to the train and go on to do the marketing. Your husband's boss may not be taking the same train., but chances are your most critical woman friends may be eyeing you bounce a melon. You have a choice of three good-looking early morning outfits.

I. Pants or shorts outfit.

Depending on the weather and whether your community accepts a leggy silhouette. Success of this outfit depends upon the cut of the pant, the length of the shorts, and the kind of top you choose, the shoes you wear, and what you do about your head.

> If slacks: Real ones, not toreador, not too tight, not above ankle-length unless you are young, slim and contemporary looking. Slacks are sensible, down-to-earth; toreador is cocktail hour. Not red, green, etc. Stick to monotones, or a conservative clan plaid. Both navy and black will show lint. Wear a tucked-in shirt or cashmere that blends, a leather or wool jacket if the weather calls for it. Shoes with low heel or no heel; but *not* ballet slippers.

> If shorts: Bermuda length, gray flannel, beige wool or a dark clan plaid or check. Shirt or tucked-in jersey or cashmere top. High socks with low-heel moccasin-type shoe. Or, if it's very hot weather, no socks and sandal or thong shoes.

> No hat and well-groomed hair preferable: Be careful about gypsy scarf arrangements to cover curlers or confusion. I can't honestly imagine any kind of hat for this kind of spotlight so you'd better have done your hair.

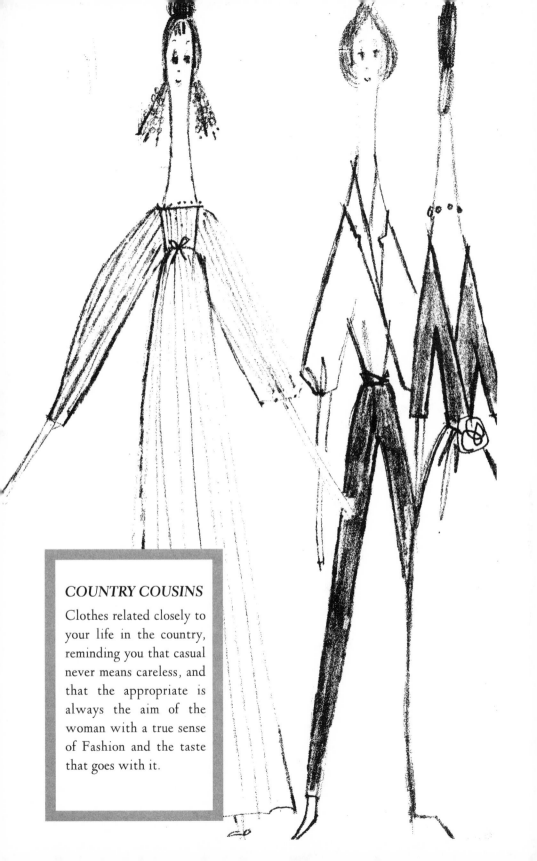

COUNTRY COUSINS

Clothes related closely to
your life in the country,
reminding you that casual
never means careless, and
that the appropriate is
always the aim of the
woman with a true sense
of Fashion and the taste
that goes with it.

II. One wonderful dress (per season).

One that doesn't remotely resemble either a Mother Hub-
bard or a dress that isn't good enough for town any more.

> For warm weather: Classic shirtwaist, belted or sashed.
> A scoop-necked sheath, not too scooped. Not a sun-
> back unless your town is very country-store casual.
> *Fabrics:* cool ones—cotton or linen. *Colors:* bright as
> you please. *Shoes:* little heels, pump or sandal. *Head-
> coverings:* small-brimmed hat, straw or piqué, if you
> like hats.

> For cooler weather: Suit; flannel or tweed or corduroy.
> Easy coat in wool or leather for really cold days. But
> please don't be all matching: tweed hat, coat, bag
> too. Too many suburbanites are.

III. Separates, for all weather, all year long.

Skirts or pants to go with vests, shirts, jackets, varied
day after day, to go to the station five days in a row, never
looking the same.

SUBURBAN P.M.

This may be the afternoon date with the other house-
wives, your most critical audience. Price-tag eyes may eye
you. Your object: to baffle (how much *did* she pay for it?); to
invite friendly envy and above all admiration. What you wear
will depend on where you go, and your part in the occasion.

"I like gardens—but not to garden in." Well, that means
you're not a down-to-earth girl, yet you like patios at the cocktail hour, designing exhibits for the Garden Club (the kind
that use driftwood and conch shells and don't necessarily have
anything to do with what you've grown yourself). So, the
clothes you associate with gardens have nothing to do with

overalls or levis or dungarees big-pocket workman aprons designed to hold trowels and scissors for pruning. You are thinking in the exact opposite of country casuals. You are looking
for clothes that are decorative, sophisticated, yet still maintain
the relaxed spirit of a cocktail hour on the terrace. Do you
want a flower print? Yes, if you can compete with the flower
garden. Perhaps one sheer bold flower color may be more effective. Brilliant pink or nasturtium orange, for instance. Do
you want pants that aren't working pants? Perhaps. And these
are the opposite of monotone train-meeting pants. Turquoise
velveteen or stark black topped with a dazzling white silk
shirt. Patio living is close to hostess living and America accepts
pants for the lady of the house—providing the pants are well-
cut, and providing the lady is practically figureless.

Garden club blue ribbon day.

You are hatted and gloved for this one, unless it's a very
intimate and informal garden club. Decide to be pretty—or
bold. The latter will cause comment, even gossip, so you must
be very sure of yourself to carry it off. By bold, I mean dramatic, new-new: a line that no one has seen anywhere except
on the Dior mannequin, the color combination that is unprece-
dented in your circles. If you're the hostess on Garden Club
Day, you may wear the kind of thing you can't wear one step
beyond the door—long jersey or chiffon, a hostess gown that
will set you completely apart.

If you decide to be pretty, choose a pastel or flower
print—not stripes or polka dots or shock colors. And don't
be afraid of the traditional garden-party hat. More and more
women are wearing them.

A restaurant date in the city.

Decide on one wonderful dress, either boldly sophisticated or conservative, but don't choose a tweed suit with
everything matching. Avoid coats, because they are cumber-
some; or little furs, too conventional. Try for unexpected

shawl stoles or bright little boleros. Be sure to be thought-out, from hat to shoes, if you have a restaurant date. Thought-out means a weather eye on, not only your umbrella but the gloves and shoes that match the season.

SUBURBAN DINNER HOUR

I. Outdoor barbeque or indoor buffet.

Cocktails on the terrace may precede either one. Pants and shirt for really rugged fireplace kind of food—steaks, big stew in an iron pot. If you start the party outside but continue indoors, you must find a happy mixture of clothes that can sit on dampish garden chairs and look unmussed when they walk around the buffet. Here is where lightweight wool jersey serves you well. And with a scooped neckline, practically backless, it will still be cool enough for summer evenings.

II. Small but dressy neighborhood dinner party.

Country living means making your own entertainment, especially during the winter months when getting to the city is difficult. While dinner parties may be small and casual, you will still want to feel festive. You'll need the kind of long dinner dress that can also be worn to the country club formal—pretty prints and pastel chiffons for summer, bright wool jersey for cold months.

III. Big evening in town.

This can mean many things—the theater and supper in the dress that looks dressed up but can match a man in a dark suit. Next, black-tie dress—short or long but not too bare and often with its own jacket which can come off. Then white-tie dress—real dancing dresses for this very formal occasion. I think they should be long but Dior doesn't always agree. They should move and have fullness somewhere, if only a fishtail. They can be slim in chiffon or silk jersey and full in taffeta or silk or velvet or brocade. They must be your most becoming and glamorous dresses. Every woman, no matter what her size and shape, may be beautiful at a ball if she thinks about herself. Some women may need the Hope diamond. But nevertheless don't be a mouse in white-tie surroundings.

CITY LIVING

Because life in America is more and more casual, even the woman who lives in the city can check her wardrobe and find many outfits adaptable to different hours and occasions. Her problem is not very different from the woman who lives in the suburbs. Outdoor barbeques may not enter into her life but hostess pants do, the same kind of hostess pants her country cousin is wearing. They will be well-cut. She will be sure before she buys them that she has the figure to wear them. She will own some shorts, for weekend visits and perhaps a Saturday morning cleaning. She won't need cabaña dresses or garden work clothes but she will wear easy suits and casual separates to market, just as they do in White Plains.

She will need far more round-the-clock clothes, especially if she has a job to go to. And here the piece wardrobe serves her most strategically. A jacket covers a bare-top during the day, comes off when she goes on to a dinner date. Jewelry is switched to show that it is after five. A short skirt is exchanged for a long one. She can quick-change as efficiently as a fireman if her piece wardrobe has been selected carefully.

She has far more temptations to make mistakes. The big-time city newspapers beguile her with advertisements. She reads all the fashion magazines and may be lured by the straw in the wind that is destined to blow away. She is aware of many choices because she understands the vocabulary of the Fashion business. She is the first to know about new trends. Right now she is packing away her small hats and investing in real hats because this is the year when hats have gone back to fitting heads. She likes them. Her hair doesn't blow—it's a new feeling.

Psychology is responsible for trends. What we have too

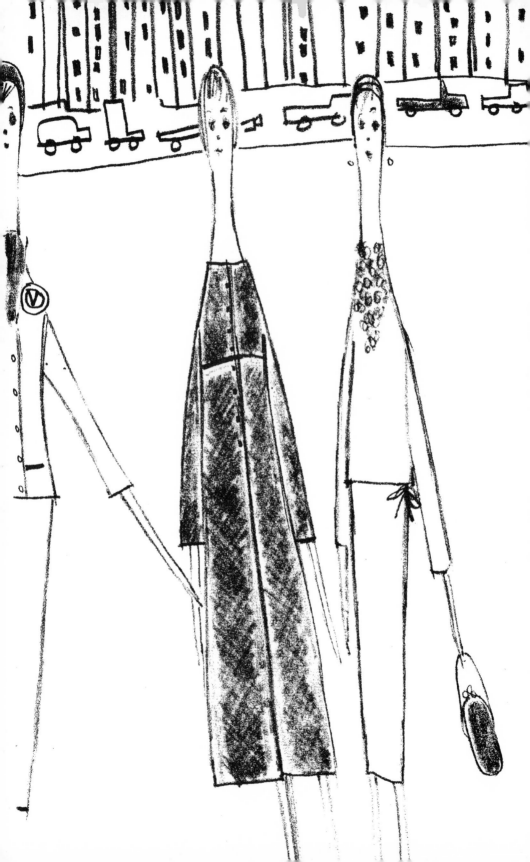

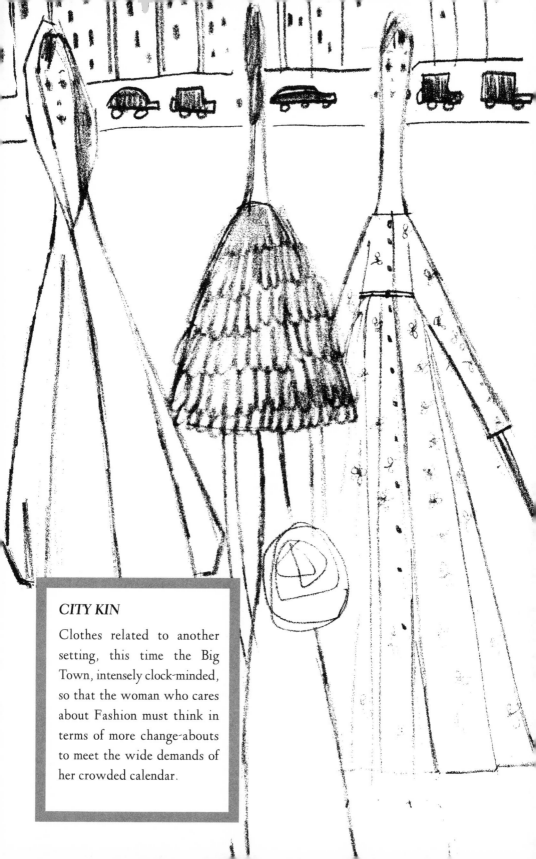

CITY KIN

Clothes related to another setting, this time the Big Town, intensely clock-minded, so that the woman who cares about Fashion must think in terms of more change-abouts to meet the wide demands of her crowded calendar.

much of today, we can't endure tomorrow. The pendulum always swings. Simplicity is spectacular in one year—and dowdy in the next. In Fashion we must always look for the woman who is happy about living in her time. She makes the proper use of progress in her clothes, wearing the newest. Fashion changes as if they had always been there.

There is an art in all this. You must never look as if you were wearing a dress for the first time, trying out a new handbag, trying to get used to a different hat shape. The uneasy look of a husband often cancels out all your brave efforts. Don't be a nervous innovator—you will never in the world start a trend.

Know how to handle the scarf, the fur, the boutonniere—or forget it. How you carry a bag, an unbrella, a glove is more important than the Fashion itself. Some women give the impression they are about to lose everything—handkerchiefs and gloves drop to the floor, umbrellas get separated from them.

Analyze heel heights. The trend is usually flexible, low ones *and* high ones. Look at your own foot. How do you walk in this shoe, that one? Find the right last, the most becoming shape.

Find the best way to anchor a hat, with sewed-in combs, with bicycle clips, or with pretty hatpins. Your hair, its texture, how you wear it, will tell you which is best for you. Comb or clips are best for fine silky hair. Hatpins slip or don't anchor. But today, at last, you can wear a hat that fits your head, solving all these problems.

Be careful about what goes under your suit. You will unbutton the jacket sometime during the day, perhaps even take it off. Take your skirts to a good tailor and have him line them so they won't spring or sag.

Think of yourself as an Abstract—down to essentials—a quick impression of highlights. Decide what you want to highlight and put your clothes emphasis right there.

What *can't* you wear? The answers to this question are important. Your coloring will give you cues. Your figure will decide for you. Your way of life will make certain prohibitions.

The ideal fashion figure has little in common with Venus

de Milo. Miss America knows that bustline and hipline must be approximately the same, and that waistline must be at least ten inches less. If your waistline is only seven inches less than your bustline, you must decide at once against wide belts. If your ribcage protrudes, a skin-tight sheath will accent the disturbing line. Look at the long length of leg that the Fashion artist draws—only one woman in thousands can match it in reality. Use a measuring tape and a mirror and a scale to understand your figure and to see where it can be improved.

This year's beau may account for changes in your wardrobe. Does he take you to lunch at the Club or at the Museum of Modern Art? The first date calls for city restaurant clothes, the smart touch of eight-button length gloves, beautiful shoes, a handsome bag, the gleam of jewelry. The second date will find you surrounded by art students, art lovers. Their clothes will be casual, often bohemian. You will feel overdressed if you look like a page from a glossy Fashion magazine.

After you have made a list of *Nos*, start a list of *Musts*. Your job, where you live, what you like yourself best in. Now take an inventory of what you own and be positive about what to keep, what to discard. How long is it since you made a real inventory of your bureau drawers, your clothes closet? You know that your linen closets are in order with enough sheets and pillowcases, guest towels for parties, blankets for cold weather. You know that your kitchen is adequately stocked with pots and pans and everyday china and fine china and silver. Can you be just as relaxed about your glove wardrobe, shoe wardrobe, supply of lingerie?

Too many women operate on the catch-as-catch-can basis, dashing out to buy stockings because they are down to the last run. Begin a systematic replacement job right now. If you can't afford to add to your wardrobe right now, try "making over" something. Wander through the piece-goods department. One exciting print can reline a suit and make you feel as if you have a brand-new outfit. Convert a high neckline into a scoop neckline. You have an entirely different dress.

Be positive in your choices. Find the most becoming shape

and stick to it. Decide on basic colors and keep them firmly in mind, even if you are only shopping for handkerchiefs. Don't waver or hesitate or postpone. The girl in the song who couldn't say "Yes" and couldn't say "No" could never have been a trend-setter. If you're a thrush—be one. But maybe you've typed yourself wrong. A peacock is, after all, a very special bird.

CHAPTER 8

DON'T LET THE DRESS RUN AWAY WITH YOU

WHEN A DRESS RUNS away with a woman, it's a horror. Think of women you know who are slaves to sequins and glitter and shiny satin and lush velvet—all hard to live up to, outsparkling the sparkle in your eyes and the glossy sheen of your hair,

Do you really understand the cruelty of a dress that is too tight for you, calling attention to figure faults? Or the too-short hemline that shows a bulging calf? Or the pinching shoe that makes your instep swell?

Not only you but your audience will be embarrassed if the clothes you wear seem to call attention to themselves.

The term "American Look" has become part of our Fashion vocabulary in recent years and it is a term we can be proud of. It is a clean-line look, just the opposite of too much dress. It is a comfortable look, neither threatening to burst at the seams nor to smother the wearer. I am always pleased when the fashion writers link my designs with the "American Look."

I have never deliberately sketched out a certain look and thought of it as American, but every collection I designed is planned for a thoroughly American way of life. I don't want to look like a royal princess or a world-famous hostess because I don't live in a palace and my dinner parties are for six, not sixty. I would feel foolish and uncomfortable sitting in a taxi with a train draped around my neck to keep it from getting dirty. Great elegance still has its place in many parts of the world, but I believe that simple elegance is here to stay in America.

The word *functional* is another good American term. It describes our modern furniture, our built-in cupboards. It also describes the clothes that are designed for our busy working and playing schedules. Isn't it sensible to match jackets to dresses, to be worn or left off according to the temperature? Isn't it useful to have quick-drying bathing suits that never come back from the weekend a soggy mess? Isn't it wonderful to unpack wool jersey and thumb your nose at an iron?

When a dress runs away with you it takes up too much of your time, tries your patience, proves disappointing in endless ways. How can you guard against this kind of mistake?

First, look at the tag describing the fabric. Will the dress wash without shrinking? Are there special instructions about cleaning or pressing? Is it color-fast? Can you afford the multiple cleaning bills that a nonwashable pastel promises?

Next look at the details of the dress. Fabric-covered buttons may have to be removed when the dress is cleaned. Is the skirt permanently pleated? Repleating is expensive. Is the piqué collar stitched around the neckline asking for trouble. It will take a good hour to take it off and sew it back on again.

Now take a final look at the dress as a dress. Are you going to be a slave to it? Is it hard to live up to? Has it identifying features you will get tired of? I am thinking of a certain black crepe dress with a stand-up mandarin collar scrolled in gold. Very memorable. Easy to tire of. Also of a well-cut suit adorned with appliqué, impossible to get rid of.

Flexibility is a word that belongs to the American Look. And *excitement*. Our lives are tuned to ingenuity—in inventions, gadgets. We like amusing surprises—Shakespeare in modern dress, opera in English, Steinberg cartoons, the unexpected in an advertising layout. Every designer on Seventh Avenue tries for excitement in every collection. We all have our special "thing." One designer likes to combine leather with fabric; another likes foreign themes. I have mine—some frankly for fun. The diaper bathing suit, blue-jean stitching, work-clothes grippers used for fastening, colored zippers meant to show, spaghetti ties. The surprise of color with color. Each new collection starts with the idea of comfort, need, fun. I am influenced by anything, everything—the ballet I just saw, an old engraving, what fabrics are doing. A T-square lying on my husband's drawing board sent me to my yellow pad and the T-square of 1954 is the result—a squared off jacket, half one color, half another.

The inspiration for the "American Look" comes from you. You, demanding more change-abouts than women did thirty years ago when a cotton house dress, an afternoon dress and something for a formal party did the trick. You, with your full life, at home, at work, on the weekend. You, looking younger for your family, and slimmer for yourself. You, enjoying clothes that are comfortable and easy to take care of.

I sit in a tiny cubbyhole above Seventh Avenue with pencil in hand, and little stick figures gradually begin to walk across the pages of my sketchbook. I snip swatches, hold fabric to the light; pull it, bias-wise, pleat it, crumple it. The fabric is my next best inspiration after you. Next to my office is a sewing room where the stick figures are transformed into working models. We—all of us—sewing and snipping, eyeing and changing things around, quarrel cheerfully about what kind of fastenings, a pocket here or there. The dress forms stand patiently, hour after hour. Then we're suddenly all satisfied and ready to cut and get going. Across the hall, the cutters are at work. They say they like the bright colors they're cutting.

Sometimes I remember my first experience with dress-making—Miss Annie who came to the house to make clothes for mother and me. The process fascinated me from the start—selecting the pictures of dresses in the *Vogue Pattern Book*, the fabrics to be bought at the dry-goods store, the cutting and basting and fitting, the pockets and buttons and buttonholes, old things made over. I soon learned the tricks of making over all my clothes each season to keep them looking like the fashion magazines said they should look. Most of the changes in Fashion are changes in fitting—waistlines, hemlines, necklines, sleeve lengths, all possible to change.

So, as far back as then, I suppose, I was formulating a philosophy about clothes, wanting them to be easy and generous and not too machined, wanting them to *look* like current Fashion even if they had to be made over to seem new. Today, my workroom knows that there are certain inviolable rules. Buttons must button. Sashes must not only tie, but be generous enough to wind round and round again, to be tied wherever the wearer wishes. I disagree with Gertrude Stein's idea of immutability: "A rose is a rose is a rose." A sash is a sash is a sash? Nonsense. I can think of it floating through a whole series of change-abouts to answer the tastes and shapes of a thousand women.

CHAPTER 9

DRESSING UP AND
DRESSING DOWN

CLOTHES HAVE MOODS. Fabrics have personalities. Prints suggest types. Colors shout or speak softly. Necklines, like history, have dates. Sleeves have, too. And you, being a woman of many moods and more than one personality to match your versatile life, will need more than one kind of clothes in your wardrobe.

I should like to take you to a specific collection and let you see for yourself the themes and the variations on the themes, suggesting always the eternal feminine but the eternal feminine in many guises.

The model enters, walking as models do, with a swing to her walk and her head held high, and pushed a little forward below the waist because she is so slender it doesn't matter. You haven't got her figure, but you might take a few cues from the way she walks. She isn't shuffling along. Her head isn't the forward part of her—it's the high part, making her look taller. She looks alert, happy, challenging, the way a woman looks when she's going to a job she likes or a date she's looking forward to. She's wearing a four-piece outfit—does that sound bulky? You can be sure it fits her perfectly. This is a dressed-down look. The colors and the style are conservative. Brown linen straight skirt, small-check cotton blouse (brown on white), red linen weskit and neutral color linen free-swinging jacket. She is wearing eight-button brown kid gloves and she is hatless. Her necklace is of big round beads, red and tortoise shell, with a tiny glitter of gold in between to match the rim of her specs.

She's the way you might like to look on a summer day on the way to your job.

The next model has a polka dot chiffon bow tied under her chin—the bows are always becoming. The suit is dark, dull green, silk linen. It is in three pieces; slim skirt with slit pockets on the hip bones, sleeveless bolero blouse, a waist-length jacket lined with the polka dot chiffon. This is the kind of suit I think is a good investment. It takes black accessories—shoes, hat and bag—because some of the polka dot pattern is black. But because the ground of the polka dot is white, white gloves crushed at the wrist look wonderful. The jacket sleeve is three inches above the wristbone allowing room for the gloves and bracelets. The same suit with a yellow sweater instead of the bolero blouse could look well in the country.

The next model is dressed for the theater in a rose and turquoise patterned coat—the fabric has a lovely damask dull finish, the texture looks antique and rich. The coat is very simply cut—no collar, no cuffs—only two slit pockets and stone buttons that match the neckline beads of turquoise and rose (many strands and many sizes of beads). The coat is lined with wool jersey in turquoise the shade of the dress. The dress is rather low-necked; no sleeves; high-waisted; with swallow-tail fullness in the back; pockets under the swallow-tail.

Next comes a silk twill dress in a daring color combination. First, the cut is simple, bias bodice, high V-neckline, buttons down the front the color of amber, full shirred skirt (it opens far enough for you to step into it), pockets on side seams, as almost always, a big long bias sash—doubled and long enough to wrap around waist three times, or try it once with a big bow, or try it with a knot, ends flying. After all it's your dress; it's made for you to wear it as you like it best. Note the colors; the skirt orange; the bodice purple; the sash bright pink—a wonderful color combination for hot days or hot countries.

Next, a dress-shirt-type dress, long, a dress to wear to

dine at home, a relaxed comfortable kind of dress that can sit cross-legged on the floor if necessary and still look sissy and pretty and proper and functional, all at one time. It can even go to dinner parties quite nicely and it will probably be more relaxing for the wearer than a tight black satin sheath that keeps her worrying about her posture all through dinner. This dress is usually in a rugged fabric—cotton or wool or silk twill—usually a fabric that you don't expect in a dinner dress, often a gay stripe or a bright plaid or an unusual color combination. Sometimes it has a shirtwaist top, sometimes it has long sleeves, sometimes it has a low neck and no sleeves at all. It is the comfortable look and the fabric that separates it from other dresses and I think you may agree that it is a for-ever dress—a real collector's item and I promise you dinner will taste better in this kind of easy, pretty outfit.

A dress with its own coat is a luxury—with the slim sil-houette and the high waistline it gives great importance to an outfit that might be very dull. In most cases the coat is more important than the dress—the dress is the background for the cut and shape and fashion in the coat. One I am think-ing of is made in a printed wool challis, shades of orange and red outlined in black and white—stitched in black with black button. Both dress and coat are in the same fabric; the coat lined in orange jersey.

Wrap and tie dresses, another comfort and joy to wear. Wrap and high-tie today or low-tie tomorrow. Always have one in black wool jersey, it's the best foil for necklaces, pins, bracelets that you can imagine. It is never the same on any two women because, as you tie it, it becomes your dress—the way you wear it makes the difference.

Those two great stand-bys, stripes and polka dots, de-mand something of your figure, but you can always find up-and-down stripes if you feel that horizontal stripes make you look wide—and while a coin dot may seem too much, polka dots, scattered or small, are easy to wear. Prints appear to pose problems they don't need to. You are frankly size 20 so you feel if you do buy a print it must be a small or over-all

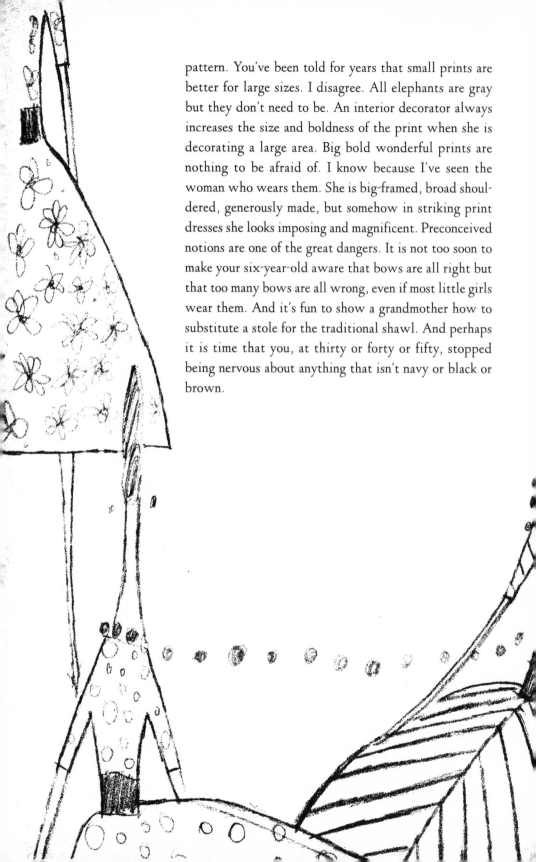

pattern. You've been told for years that small prints are better for large sizes. I disagree. All elephants are gray but they don't need to be. An interior decorator always increases the size and boldness of the print when she is decorating a large area. Big bold wonderful prints are nothing to be afraid of. I know because I've seen the woman who wears them. She is big-framed, broad shouldered, generously made, but somehow in striking print dresses she looks imposing and magnificent. Preconceived notions are one of the great dangers. It is not too soon to make your six-year-old aware that bows are all right but that too many bows are all wrong, even if most little girls wear them. And it's fun to show a grandmother how to substitute a stole for the traditional shawl. And perhaps it is time that you, at thirty or forty or fifty, stopped being nervous about anything that isn't navy or black or brown.

I think by now you can spot dressed-up and dressed-down costumes just as well as I can. I am sure you can figure out why gold self-dotted satin is a dress-up dress; why white silk sprigged with tiny roses is just as effective in its way, but not in the same way as gold satin. Why do I put big pearl buttons on avocado polka dot satin? To let you be frankly dressed up. Why do I choose a luxurious silk print in shades of dark greens and blacks? To keep you subtly dressed down. A simple summer sleeveless dress may want to stay in the background. If it doesn't, put big gold beads on the shoulders, holding back and front together. A shirt may want to be s conservative man-tailored affair. If it doesn't, alternate the buttons, using one of one kind, one of another. The effect is amusing and not at all masculine. Thong sandals make city dresses look casual; pastel doeskin gloves make cottons look city. This is another way to dress up and dress down.

CHAPTER 10

DISCIPLINE OF CLOTHES

WHEN YOU STOP to think how important clothes can be, you gain a new respect for them. The right dress may get you a job, win you a beau, or a vote, or even a husband! Here they are, from hat to shoe, each and all together a subtle adding or subtracting of you. Clothes can't be neglected without attracting attention, nor overemphasized without notice. You say what you are with the clothes you wear, say it everywhere you go and to everyone you meet—your family, your friends, your boss, even to strangers on the street.

Some say: "I don't care. I know my heels are run down— I like them that way. They adjust to the way I walk, and besides nobody ever looks at them."

But *somebody* does. I once had a boss who automatically flicked imaginary lint off the suits of his employees. I am quite sure that *that* boss would register every run-down heel.

Some say: "I've thought about what I'm wearing. I'm alive and glad of it and it's worth getting up fifteen minutes earlier in the morning to be certain that that last glimpse in the mirror tells me I'm all one piece, harmonious with myself, the people I'm going to meet, the places I'm going to be."

Some say: "I've more money then I know what to do with—look at me—watch me spend it!"

And *somebody* is sure to say: "Poor thing—she's so bored she doesn't know *what* to do with herself—so she buys and buys and shops and shops and everybody knows it."

Some say: "I'm lazy and careless when it comes to broken straps and runs in my stockings but I'm a wonderful wife and mother and surely that is far more important than clothes."

But is she a wonderful wife and mother—I mean 100 per

cent wonderful? Does her husband wince at the company
party when he knows her slip is showing and that all the junior mail clerks are probably saying "Look at Mr. Big's wife—
it's snowing down there?" And will her three little girls grow
up oblivious to all the little things that count: a broken strap
sewn back on with the right color thread instead of just any
piece of thread that's handy, buttons matching when they're
supposed to, seams together, a hook to go with every eye? It
is very possible that the three little girls will notice a
mother's carelessness and become perfectionists. Then the
mother will really suffer because there will be hostility or
condescension when her negligence shows.

Some say: "I'm so dowdy and so refined..." You can see a
world of far-too-proper Bostonians and drab figures holding
on to an unbecoming dress "because it's still good—and that's
more important than style."

Do you agree when I say it is *not* refined to offend people's
sensibilities, to defy the laws of grace and beauty, to impose
ugliness?

Some say: "I've just discovered Dior—I'll wear it all at
one time."

And at this I have *nothing* to say, out of respect for Dior,
and all he *didn't* want the lady to do.

But a blessed some say: "I can wear it and I know how to
wear it and when and where it belongs."

And these are fewer than they need to be because every
woman can get up fifteen minutes earlier, can learn to focus
her eyes on details, can discover the fundamentals that make
well-dressed women.

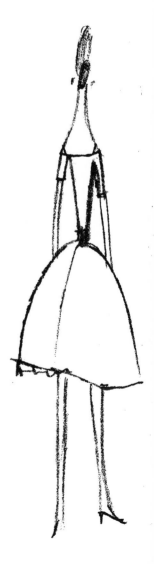

Sometimes clothes steal the scene
with no applause.

Don't let things wave, signal, stop both you and the
show. A hat with a feather flying in the wind—and an expression of acute anxiety on the wearer as she wonders
whether the feather can take it. The scarf that may blow in

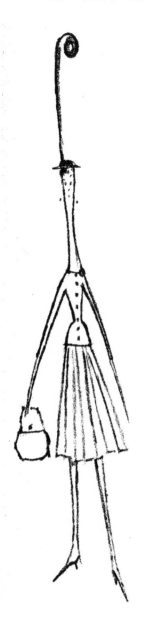

your face and blind you as you ride horseback or go sailing or try to cross a street with lots of traffic on a near-hurricane day. Pleated skirts that can't stay put when there's a sixty-mile gale.

I am saying what a good mariner says when the winds are high: "Batten down the hatches—batten down everything on the boat." Remember, clothes—like sails—don't stand still.

Nobody wants to look as if they are quite literally blowing apart. The hat that goes sailing across the street always makes the poor owner a figure of fun.

Pocketbook discipline.

Be careful about what comes out of your pocketbook. This may include musty-looking powder puffs, unpaid bills, the odds and ends of tissues, bobby pins, and the notes you write to yourself. A pocketbook can remind you of just how lax you are being with yourself. Do you taken down people's telephone numbers and addresses and fail to transfer them to your address book? They will expect to hear from you eventually, you know—and what happens when it's Christmas-card time? Memory is not infallible. A scrawled number that has lived like a mole in the zipper compartment of your bag may mean little or nothing when you chance upon it on a cleaning-out day.

What is allowed in? Coin purse, billfold, driver's license, identification cards. Compact, lipsticks (more than one shade), eye shadow, mascara. Small leather case containing scissors, nail file, emery board. Small address book, with a stampbook tucked inside. Pencil, pen, pocket-comb, mirror, checkbook, keys. And the fresh handkerchief you put in before you leave the house.

What gets in and shouldn't. This is a television joke. I wouldn't attempt to make a list. It might include anything from pictures of distant relatives to an old grocery list or keys that don't fit anything in your life.

Try to buy leather-lined bags, easy to clean. Shake out loose tobacco leaves and powder, wipe with a damp cloth. And remember you alone can discipline your pocketbook, see that it *stays* clean and uncluttered.

Keep it clean.

In this new world of quick-drying fabrics, looking fresh and feeling fresh is easy. Find a cleaner you can trust, but don't expect miracles. He may be unfamiliar with the best way to treat leather and suede, so you will have another name in your address book, the specialist who knows how. If you are sending stretchable or shrinkable clothes, give the cleaner exact measurements, length from waist to shoulders, from waist to hem, and exact waist measurements also. And when the clothes return from the cleaners don't undo all the care you've taken by hanging them on flimsy wire hangers. Fold sweaters professionally, just as they came from the store, and lay them flat in a drawer or chest. Loop knitted dresses through the rung of a wooden hanger, distributing the weight evenly. Don't let a black jersey get next to a fuzzy tweed—if it does, by accident, use strips of Scotch tape to remove the lint from the jersey. And look at shoes. Do keep leather polished, heels straight.

Dress up for yourself—best discipline of all.

You are spending the evening alone and the temptation is to say "Off with my town clothes into any old thing." Trailing around in an old flannel bathrobe isn't going to make you feel relaxed. Glimpsing a shiny nose in the mirror isn't going to build your morale. Use a small part of this precious evening for making yourself look pretty. Invest in at least one cozy and beautiful house coat. Mine is tomato-red jersey, clinging, warm, *long*. The point is lost if you are looking pretty "in case somebody drops in." You are dressing up for *yourself*. Obviously you can't dash in the house and slip on something pretty

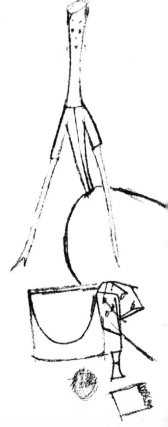

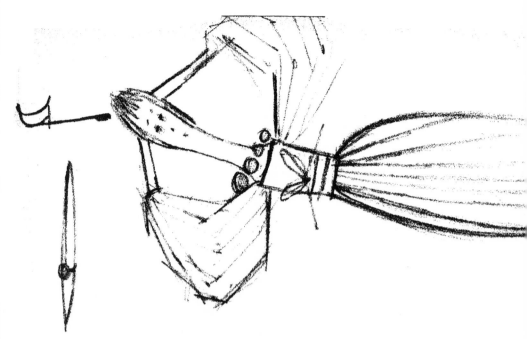

if there aren't any glamorous things in your wardrobe. So don't let all your nightgowns and peignoirs go at once. Keep a strict inventory on mules, scuffs, warm bedroom slippers. More than one bedjacket if you like reading in bed. To *feel* luxurious, you must look luxurious.

The moment you find yourself saying to yourself, "Nobody ever sees me in this old bathrobe except my husband"—toss out the bathrobe. Some things stay in your collection forever—and shouldn't. I have never liked that old saying, "Comfortable as an old shoe." An old shoe may give the illusion of comfort but may at the same time be doing untold harm to the bones in your feet. "But," you may argue, "it's still wearable. It would be extravagant to throw it away."

What is extravagance? Buying more than you can afford, or just as bad, buying something you don't need or even like. Discipline yourself against this kind of extravagance, but don't confuse skimping at the wrong time or being afraid to get rid of something with thrift. Getting rid of something can be just as important as collecting. Have you ever lost track of a season? Turned up at the concert in your old winter

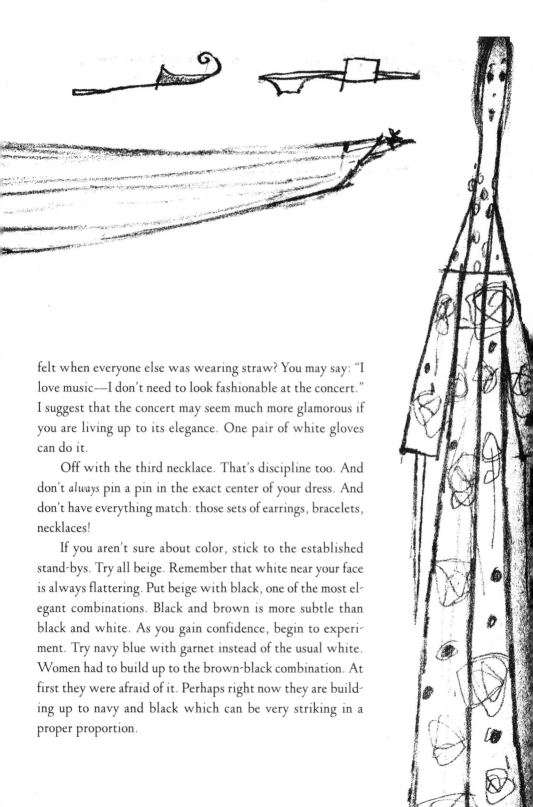

felt when everyone else was wearing straw? You may say: "I love music—I don't need to look fashionable at the concert." I suggest that the concert may seem much more glamorous if you are living up to its elegance. One pair of white gloves can do it.

Off with the third necklace. That's discipline too. And don't *always* pin a pin in the exact center of your dress. And don't have everything match: those sets of earrings, bracelets, necklaces!

If you aren't sure about color, stick to the established stand-bys. Try all beige. Remember that white near your face is always flattering. Put beige with black, one of the most elegant combinations. Black and brown is more subtle than black and white. As you gain confidence, begin to experiment. Try navy blue with garnet instead of the usual white. Women had to build up to the brown-black combination. At first they were afraid of it. Perhaps right now they are building up to navy and black which can be very striking in a proper proportion.

Too disciplined.

I am thinking now of the women who are miserable if they aren't living copies of the newest look. They have somehow confused values, are wearing themselves into a state of nerves trying to keep up with the latest Fashion headline. The result is often a canceling out of Fashion. They look too perfect. And too often with it all comes a lack of serenity that shows in spite of careful make-up and beautifully groomed hair. Please don't think of the word discipline as rigid, punishing, painful. Please keep on thinking of Fashion as fickle and silly and wonderful and unpredictable. Let it do well by you in the good sense—never be a slave to it.

CHAPTER 11

REAL SPORT CLOTHES
—OR DON'T LET THE
FISH SEE YOU

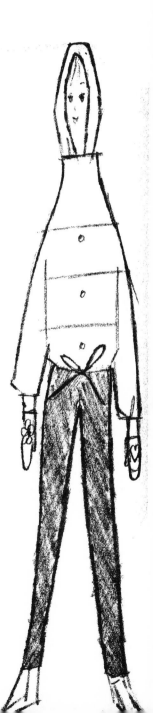

TRY NOT TO BE conspicuous if you can't ski, can't really handle a rod, don't know a trot from a canter.

Strangely enough, the clothes that go with active sports show up your background more than any other clothes. A first round of golf is often spotted *before* that first dribble off the tee. The little things that make sports clothes correct or incorrect are hardly noticeable to the newcomer, yet the mistakes made by the novice are glaring ones to the old-timer.

Nothing should look new, everything should look weatherbeaten, broken-in, even worn. That's the real evidence a sportsman looks for. Collector's items, accumulated through years of devotion to a sport, are more in tune with sports than new polish, new golf clubs, new skis, new fishing tackle. All are horrors until they look as if *you* have done something with them. The 8-iron that has never dug a divot is simply not authentic; it's a stage prop.

All sports clothes look queer when they are not in the right place. Imagine ski pants on the beach, jodhpurs on skis, a pink coat on a bicycle, skirts at a field trial, blue denim on ice—all the other nightmares. Get sound advice on sports clothes before you buy. There is no place where extravagant mistakes can be more costly, and also no place where money well-spent can be of greater advantage. Many kinds of sports clothes last a lifetime—the skiing season is short, a good leather vest will be chilly-day golf equipment year after year, the superb riding habit tailored in England is for ever. Sports

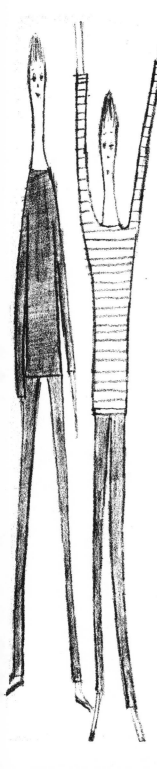

clothes designed to participate, also look queer when they are worn by spectators. Don't come to the tennis matches in a short white tennis dress unless you are going to be on the court. Riding hats are for the riders, not for those of you who hold the programs. You couldn't possibly be an active jockey so don't wear a jockey shirt.

However, certain spectator sports put you on the grounds and etiquette calls for certain conforming. You don't follow Ben Hogan in a National Open in anything but low shoes. The Golfing Fathers will order you off the course if your spike heels are digging into "their turf." You can't watch a ski match in anything but ski clothes—you'd freeze to death. On the other hand, if you are a spectator at a football game or at Ascot, you can wear your most handsome things—from beautiful tweeds to a garden hat.

Another sport caution: *above all be comfortable.* Don't be the skier who gets so cold she can't stand it and some poor soul has to leave the fun to take her back to the lodge. Don't overlook long woollen underwear. 100 per cent wool socks, hoods, mittens. Don't get your feet wet; that's a sure way to freeze. Be sure your boots are roomy to keep the blood circulating. Sometimes clothes can be *too* heavy—that can mean trouble. You can get very tired in a coat that weighs a ton. Perhaps layers of sweaters topped by a thin windbreaker will do the job, or the smart and sensible use of *real* underwear— a whole suit of it covering you like a leotard.

Avoid elaborate sports equipment, the *whole* works, if you're a beginner. And attention-getting clothes. If you're going mostly to stand and watch while you're waiting for your first ski lesson, don't be a scarlet tanager or the girl in the breathtaking skin-tight pants. Stick to navy blue with enough room to roll in when you fall. If you have just decided to take up golf, don't buy out Abercrombie's. Wait until you can get off the tee creditably before you line your belt with tees, wear a medal you've never won. Be sure your skirt it not too full; it will interfere with your putting on a windy day. Be sure your skirt is not too tight; it will make the hills you climb seem steeper. Don't buy a *scratchy* linen blouse even if it does match your skirt. Swinging a club causes friction; you'll end with a sore red skinned place as sure as anything. If your club allows shorts, be sure they are Bermuda length, and never wear slacks on a golf course unless it is a stormy day in early spring or late fall. Knee socks are correct with shorts, but because every woman wants to get her legs tanned, this nicety is sometimes overlooked. But if you do wear short socks with shorts, keep them below the shoe line, not bulging at the ankles. Color in golf shoes asks for attention. Brown, black, white or dark and white combinations look smartest. Monotone colors look handsome: grays, browns, beiges for skirt and sweater combinations. Pastels are pretty but so predominant on the golf course they begin to look commonplace. Standard headgear: visor or mushroom shape cap with small turned-down brim. Never a sunbonnet! Perhaps a beret or a tam if you're a tournament player. Golf gloves are probably the only gloves in the world that are permitted to look "worn."

There is almost no such thing as sports jewelry. The sensible reason: it is apt to get in the way of sport. Tournament golfers may wear their medals providing they don't dangle and distract: pinned at the throat or anchored to a collar is all right. Any skier is entitled to a St. Christopher medal—somewhere unobtrusive—attached to a belt or on a thin chain under your blouse. But "No" to pearls, too many rings, bracelets. If you wear a watch, be sure it is on a narrow leather band.

I am not a tennis player but I know what I like to look at: very simple short white tennis dresses without baby-doll flounces or lace-trimmed panties.

There are two types of riding clothes for two kinds of riders. Dude ranchers would feel silly in the traditional Madison Square Horse Show outfit. Levis or frontier pants with cowboy boots are completely at home on the plains. But you *don't* wear them in Central Park or in riding shows. Your child may be the best rider in suburban Connecticut but she won't

win a prize at the local show if her riding outfit isn't correct. Be sure she conforms to the rules.

The wrong shoes in the wrong place are another give-away: tennis shoes on the golf course, or worse, sandals; house slippers to bowl in; skates attached to just any old pair of shoes. Croquet is about the only sport I can think of, where you *could* wear high heels and a dress-up dress.

Do you swim? Do you dive? Do you just get your feet wet? Do you sit all day on the sand or beside the pool? Do you tan or sunburn or are you a pale pink type? Designers of bathing suits and beach togs have had all of you in mind as they set about transforming American seascapes into scenes as colorful as Dufy's.

We've come a long way from Annette Kellerman, the first to begin to free the bathing suit. But sometimes we've gone backward. I am afraid that little-girl dresses worn as bathing suits suggest retrogression.

I like to swim. I like bathing suits made of lightweight wool jersey with necklines that can move around and not mark my sunburn. I hate wet skirts sticking to wet bodies. Little-girl frills, so sweet *before* you touch the water, can look very drowned-rattish as they walk back to the umbrella. Don't think you are covered up with that frilly skirt. Those ruffles may do a covering job when they are dry but you're still underneath for wet cotton to stick to. Why not wear wool jersey in the first place? You have a better chance of looking the same when you come out of the water as when you went in.

On the other hand, if you're only a sitter, not a get-wet-ter, look as pretty as possible. But remember gold and lamé look better under the moon. Prettiest of all may be a stark black suit, cut to make you look slimmer, especially smart with a tanned body. Sharp white is also effective but hard to wear if your skin has been completely protected by a parasol. Fabric is to me all-important, both in swimming and under the umbrella. I prefer unshiny materials: knits, smooth wool, dull-surfaced cottons. The suit that gives the illusion of one piece is most flattering. If not the *maillot* (all in one piece), a suit cut on Princess lines, with or without a skirt. Pants and separate tops demand a midriff absolutely above reproach. Modesty in a bathing suit is dependent on your figure. You can be completely covered and still look immodest if you aren't careful about the style of the suit, how it is cut, the firmness of the fabric. New power fabrics, many of them used for girdles, help your figure. Dark colors underemphasize. But don't wear bathing suits that look like foundation garments. And remember your back is always with you, even in a bathing suit.

When it's cover-up time, if you've had enough sun, if you feel chilly, there are dozens of interesting choices. Capes, comfortable to put on and take off easily, man-tailored terry-cloth shirts, smock-type coats—mine is called the T-Square— mandarin jackets, the conventional long coat-robe that ties shut. Your tendency to burn may make the long robe a neces-sity. The shorter jackets are more attractive if you have pretty tanned legs because somehow beach is associated with the leggy look of sea birds.

Don't expect to look glamorous in a bathing cap unless you have chiseled features and can wear your hair skinned back. But after all you don't have to *sit* in a bathing cap. Off with it the minute you emerge from that dive. Young girls swimming with no caps and wet hair plastered Audrey Hep-burn style or trailing à la mermaid look natural and unclut-tered but the no-cap method is not for everyone. Think of bathing caps as utilitarian to protect your ears, keep your hair at least semi-dry. Bathing-cap designers have not improved cap construction very much in the last ten years. I think we need more becoming shapes, tight around the edge but with room inside for hair so that it will not be completely flat-tened. One designer has come up with frankly real-hat styles: the helmet with trimming, a flower toque. Other imitate wigs with raised grooved curls. If you look nice in them, they're fun.

Wear beach shoes if you are unpedicured. I don't mean

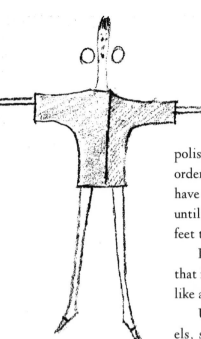

polish on your toenails necessarily. I do mean cuticle in order. Hide crooked toes, any disfigurements. But if you have beautiful feet, don't bother about sandals or scuffs until you walk to the car. Nothing is prettier than pretty feet tanned to match tan legs.

If you wear a hat, make it big and bold—a real hat that is an umbrella in itself. But never anything that looks like a garden party.

Unattractive at beach or pool: frayed or faded towels, small and skimpy-looking, suggesting they are no longer good enough for your own bathroom; city handbags or transparent plastic. Bring a straw basket that water won't hurt or a drawstring pouch crocheted out of heavy twine. Use a plaid cloth or navy-blue duffle bag to tote home damp towels and suits; never city luggage. The idea is to look uncluttered, free and easy, un-damp, natural as sun and air.

Sailing, either on a dinghy or somebody's yacht, suggests similar wardrobes. Pants, long ones. The motion of the boat asks for them. You can roll them up for a tan, pull them down if you are in a calm sea drifting in the broiling sun for hours. For the same reason, you need arm covering. A man-type shirt with sleeves that can be rolled up is good. If you want to wear a mariner's short-sleeved

T-shirt, be sure you have an extra jacket along. The best colors are navy, faded blue, white. Somehow bright green or red looks out of place in your "blue" surroundings. Leave middies, stars, anchors and gold braid to the crew and the owner—there is something musical comedy about such trappings when sailing is not your "business."

Top-siders, those safe rubber-soled shoes that cling to the deck, are essential.

A scarf to keep your hair from flying is one kind of headgear, but hair looks pretty flying and perhaps you can skin it back and tie it, or tuck some of it under a small navy or black flannel beret.

You'll need a weatherproof jacket or coat in case you run into a squall or if you're racing through high waves. Don't go sailing if you are afraid of the water. Your fears will show in your face and spoil not only your fun but the fun of the others. This is nothing to be ashamed of. Some people are afraid to ride horses. Some shiver at the hazards of skiing. But somewhere there should be *some* sport that suits you perfectly. Exercise and recreation are the answer to many things—an antidote for today's tensions, a beauty treatment, a great preventer of doctor's bills. Plus, of course, the fun of a whole extra wardrobe designed to make you comfortable and pretty while you play.

CHAPTER 12

JOURNEY PROUD

B AGGAGE FOLLOWS THE same rules as sports equipment. Where have those bags been? This is the all-important thing. They shouldn't look as if they've only been sitting in your closet. I don't mean stickers from Niagara Falls. I mean beaten-up in the good sense, lived-with on boats and trains and in auto trunks. When you look at the bags put up on the customs counters you can almost match the people and bags as each traveler comes to claim his own. The too-blonde lady *would* want pink leather, and the minute the bags reach her hotel you can be quite sure she will put on their drab cases and all that pink glory will be hidden. There are all sorts of small revealing touches. How are the bags monogramed. In blaring too-big gilt letters or with small discreet initials burned in the leather, toning in with it, not looking like an advertisement? One of the smartest women I know, famous for her understated and severe but feminine clothes, owns black leather bags, the *unshiny* black of dull kid. On the top of a taxi in France, I saw a most beautiful collection of luggage—brown canvas, lightweight, pigskin edges and frames, with the name of the masculine owner written in bold letters on each bag. The bags were many sizes and shapes, but all of the same make and design. I am sure that one carried shoes, one hats, one shirts, one socks, ties, handkerchiefs, one suits, one sports clothes, the way it should be done. So dream of finding some such perfection in your smaller forty pounds.

You expect a man to carry leather luggage, well-worn with a traveled where-has-he-been, where-is-he-going look. Leather itself is not heavy; it is the backing and frames and unnecessary construction put in luggage that makes it heavy. It can be bought with soft construction, good locks and straps. There are other choices. Imitation leather—never. You might just as well be seen with a cardboard suitcase. Light aluminium frames covered with denim, navy blue with red leather border stripe for instance. Bright colored plastic bags—*never*. But striped canvas looks travel-worthy.

Plane travelers have discovered the great advantages of knapsacks and duffle bags, cloth and leather luggage made without the frames that add weight. And don't think that a bag must be equipped with coat and suit hangers, divided interiors. Actually, the larger space makes things easier to fit in. And no coat hanger in the world is going to protect the suit that was born to wrinkle. This means all stiff fabrics. Tissue paper takes up space. Roll your dresses—they line up like soldiers and come out with fewer wrinkles. Travel with clothes that can take it: jersey, good wool, cotton. Don't think that everything has to be nylon. Some nylon is a godsend but cotton can stand wear and tear and still look fine and clean. I think of those first nylon dresses that went to Europe in '52 and '53. Those poor marked women—it didn't take long for everyone to know that had only one dress to be washed each night and worn again the next day.

Going on a trip is like betting on the races—will it be hot, will it be cold, will it rain all the time, will I have a chance to wear a long evening dress, will I need shoes to walk in the mountains, or will the weather say open-toe sandals? Will everyone wear hats or will a scarf do just as well?

It takes imagination to pack for a trip. Dream about the things that will *never* happen—they *might*. You might be invited to the Queen's garden party; you might have a chance to visit the Pope. You might be asked to a real party or a gala opera performance where anything shorter than long is frowned on. In spite of all the advice of travel agencies, take one long dress, you never know when you'll need it until the hour arrives. And imagine being stuck in your cotton skirt and shirt at such a time!

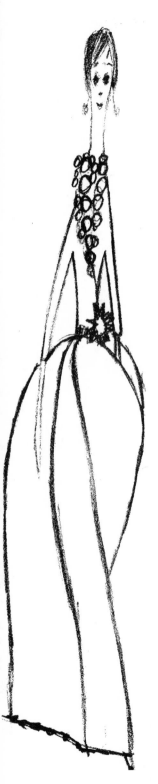

Paris has sidewalks just like New York. And buses and taxicabs. The shoes you wear all day in New York will be fine for all day in Paris. But are you really going to go to all those museums? You are. So you will need soft comfortable shoes. Not heavy walking shoes if you aren't accustomed to them. Too many fledglings seem to think that plans for Europe begin with a pair of heavy sensible shoes.

There are so many kind of trips and twenty rules could be written and still not cover everything, but there are certain procedures that will simplify planning for any trip. There are trips with Thomas Cook when you need one skirt, some blouses, one nightgown and a pair of walking shoes. There are trips that take you to only one place and you will find out what you need for that place—what kind of people you will be with, what kind of life you will lead there. There are trips when you go to many places, where you need beach clothes, evening clothes, city clothes—lists such as this.

Dresses	Shorts
Suits	Slacks
Blouses	Bathing Suits
Sweaters	Stockings
Scarves	Shoes
Bags	Gloves
Hats	Jewelry
Underwear	

To make lists is fun and certainly great insurance against reaching your destination with something important missing. The best way is to start with a general list, like the one above, adding notes to it. Dresses-city, dresses-country, and how many. And so on down through each item. Next, toss everything you own on the bed and begin to separate the essentials from things you can leave behind. See what goes with what. Do you have the right shoes for the dinner dress? Do you have the sandals for the bathing suit? Did you pack the white gloves for the black suit?

Travel, as I have told you before, was my first inspiration when I began to design a five-piece wardrobe that could stretch around and look different for different occasions. The ideal piece-wardrobe for travel must have a short skirt, a long skirt, a bare top, a covered top, and a matching coat. Let this be your basic buy if you are starting out new. Everything co-ordinates, everything works together, but never all five pieces at the same time. With this as a start, begin to add—a stole or a dressed-up cashmere sweater or a scarf. A packable hat— the twist of jersey or satin for instance. Extra blouses. But remember, the five-piece wardrobe sets your color scheme. Anything you add, whether shoes or gloves or jewelry, must blend with this basic color scheme.

Weekends.

A weekend can be anything. Suppose it is a trip to an old friend, married now, with a home in the suburbs. You board a commuter train at 5.00 on Friday. When you arrive you may go for a swim, or to a cocktail party in the neighborhood. You don't really know what your hostess has in mind until you get there. But foresighted you says "Better put in bathing things." You wear something simple for dinner but it should look like dinner—not like the office. Accessories usually do the trick. Maybe you'll go to a dance at the country club, so bring a long skirt. But don't wear it if your hostess is wearing a simple informal linen.

Too few clothes can spoil a weekend. I remember one where the heat and humidity were so incredibly high it was almost impossible to get yourself dry after a shower. Every-thing wilted. The span from Friday night to Monday morning train time became a nervous kind of juggling. "I'll save this for tomorrow—no, I'll have to wear it tonight." Of course you can always borrow. But don't.

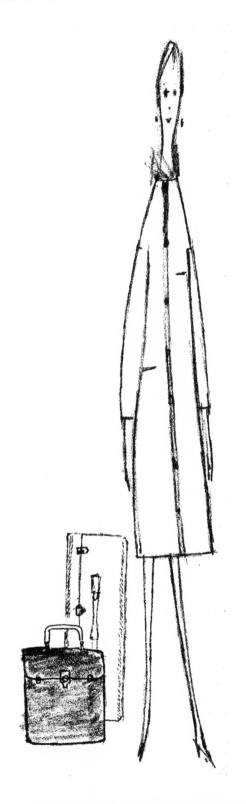

FLEXIBLE FIVE-PIECE WARDROBE SPEAKS FOR ITSELF

Designed to save luggage space, it is not only adaptable to the timed-to-the-minute datebook of the woman who goes on from her job to evening festivities—but it answers beautifully the question marks of a weekend visit where there might be an occasion when a long skirt would be really missed.

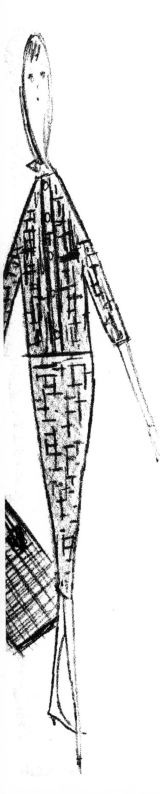

In the public eye.

Don't forget that the moment you leave the privacy of your own home, you are in the public eye. Travel, like the goldfish bowl, removes privacy. You are instantly subjected to the critical eye of station masters, porters, hotel clerks, stewards, bellboys. And what a really educated eye they have when it comes to appraising a traveler!

They will judge you by your luggage and predict your tip. They will judge you by your gloves—or lack of gloves. By the shine of your shoes, by the scuffed look of the old pair you decided to wear because nobody you know will be seeing you.

If you travel in black, be sure it's not crepe or satin or a cocktail dress. Black tweed, black cotton twill, black denim or the new miracle uncrushables are acceptable. Tweed is wonderful for cool climates. Leather coats, too.

If you are on an auto trip you may decide that riding is more comfortable in slacks. It is, but when you want to stop at a good restaurant you may be refused admission. And suddenly the big-city hotel has "No rooms."

All this may seem cruel, snobbish, too conventional, unreal—but travel has its codes, rather rigid ones, and if you don't conform you may be inconvenienced or downright embarrassed.

"Do we *have* to wear the navy blue again," two little girls said to their mother as they started out for the six-hour drive to Boston. "Do you want to have lunch at a nice restaurant or at a hamburger stand?" their mother replied. And because they loved the special occasion of the nice restaurant, they sighed and conformed, got into their navy-blue dresses and packed their shirts and shorts.

The public eye also includes all those strangers waiting for the same train, going up the same gangplank. It is gratifying to be looked at with appreciation and interest. "She must be somebody." Not because you are wearing an orchid—but because you are the picture of what a well-dressed, well-

equipped traveler should be. You continue to stay in the public eye on board the train or ship or plane, and here you are
seen close up. The run in your stocking that would get by in
a busy restaurant, is glaringly apparent as you sit in the club
car. Too conspicuous clothes are censured. If you're dowdy,
people feel sorry for you. If you decide to be unconventional,
do it with imagination and amusement. Try a straw suitcase.

The more you travel the more you learn to keep an eye on
your baggage and the porter. Where is he going with it and
why? Know what you have, have it well marked. Count it
often. Less luggage is lost than you think, but it can be if you
leave everything up to the porter.

You may not be the shuffleboard type, but the sun deck
is wonderful and you are going to feel silly sitting up there in
dressed-up clothes. You can leave New York in a snowstorm
and be in the Gulf Stream three days later, pining for a pair
of shorts or a sunback cotton. You can be bound for Bermuda
with trucks full of tropical clothes and run into a storm without anything protective to wear in it. A London spring without very adequate central heating is quite different from
spring in Rome with sunshine acting like a furnace. Don't take
it for granted that seasons always live up to their names—
there are different kinds of winters in New York and
Chicago.

All this means do your trouble shooting beforehand. The
idea is to keep you looking serene, feeling comfortable, the
better to show off those lovely clothes.

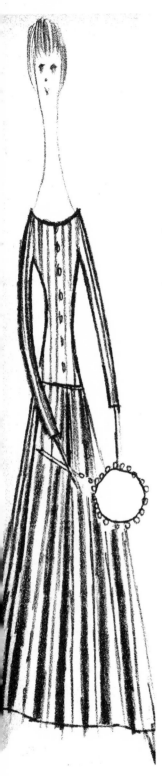

CHAPTER 13

"SHE'S USING HER BANGS FOR EYEBROWS"

THE ABOVE IS ONE of those wonderful "overheard remarks" which says so compactly what has been bothering you but you couldn't put your finger on it. The woman "they" were talking about had done nothing about eyebrows that nature had made definitely light. Obviously, she had looked in the mirror and missed seeing eyebrows. Either afraid of darkening them, or unaware that she could, she had compensated by a heavy bang of hair to take away the bald look. There can be a bald look if the face is large and the eyes are unaccented. This does not mean for one moment that I want theatrical eyes. Heavy mascara and too much eye shadow belong in the wings of Shubert Alley. But some eye make-up is a real improvement if you know how to manage it. This means drawing your *own* lines, not changing the shape your eyebrows were made in the first place. The moment you start tweezering nature away, you're asking for trouble. What you should try to do is highlight. If your eyes are small, it isn't really cheating to do something with the outer corners of your eyebrows—a tilted line or a V-shape or a round dot (on one side) pretending it's a mole. If you have circles under your eyes, darker lids will distract. If you are good with a mascara brush, do sweep up your eyelashes, making sure that there is no stiffness, no stuck look.

Color on your eyelids can be beautiful. This is what a painter does when he makes an impressionistic portrait—grayed blue or green adds becoming shadows. But I do believe in an un-made-up look, a natural look, so go lightly with all

those fascinating little brushes and jars of color. Let the fashion magazines intrigue you with sequins on eyelids, with doe
looks, mandarin looks and that wonderful dark line under the
lower lashes that is practically impossible to do. Have fun
looking, then try some of it perhaps.

To me the best look is the clean soap-and-water look.
Always look scrubbed. I like a light dusting of powder. I've
never seen a powder base that covered bad skin, bad diet.
The real skin comes from inside, not outside. And even
when your skin needs protection from the wind or the sun,
it's better to grease your face than to mask it with a powder
base.

For daily routine, a think cream base and a light dusting
of powder the color of your skin should do. Attractive lips,
like eyes, mean knowing how to draw a line and sticking to
the shape nature intended. I like light lipstick colors but
your opinion is your own. Rouge hardly exists today but if
you need it try a slight touch down the bone on your nose,
blending into your forehead, and a touch on your chin.
Remember very light touches—it brings just the glow of a
first sunburn. Use the same method when your sunburn is
not even—balance where you aren't burned with this light
touch of rouge. And when I say light I mean light—a far cry
from painted women.

Be careful about throwing yourself on the mercy of a hairdresser selling permanent waves. He can take away everything
that is you and make you a curly-haired advertisement. The
same thing applies to dye. Remember straight hair can be set
in place too. Sometimes a well-done blueprint of what you
want is a life-saver—ends curled forward or back or under,
the natural part kept. Then if you land in Dubuque or Paris
or in the beauty parlor of the *Queen Mary*, you can hand the
drawing to whomever you get and avoid worry and argument.

Never have a static hair-do. There is nothing as dull as
only one way to do your hair. Of course my preference is for
long hair—it moves, it changes. One way for sports, one way
all day, a new twist for a party. High on your head in one

mood, low on your neck in another. Never static does not mean never satisfied, always trying for something you can't be, dashing to a new hairdresser each week, hoping for a miracle. It is neurotic and childish to try to escape the facts of your age, your features, the color of your hair.

Long hair has great ability to follow fashion. You can make it look short by cutting a fluff in front or straggly bangs. You can make it look small and neat by skinning it back in an unobtrusive knot. You can wear it piled high on top, low on your neck, pony-tail for sports. I think hairdressers could profit by my theory because every woman would like to discover a new way to wear her hair with every new dress— with every new fashion trend. There would be just the "permanent" to end all troubles until the time comes for a new permanent. And speaking of permanents, why not forget them? Try setting hair as nature intended—recognize it and insist on it—make it your crowning glory. It may not be a dramatic widow's peak; it may be only a softly rounded line outlining your forehead, but whatever it is it is far more interesting than the machine kink that can make a peasant out of a wellborn lady.

Hands are another focal point so the question of what shade of polish remains with you—what red for the red suit, and Fashion says it doesn't have to match. The shape of your nails and the health of your nails are important. Consider occupational hazards when you choose your nail polish. If polish is apt to chip, use a natural polish that won't show as it wears away. There is nothing more fun, if you have the time and patience, than keeping each finger in a shining state of colorful perfection. But if you do your own dishes and normal household carpentry, or if you type all day, it is almost impossible to keep perfect nails without day-to-day attention. Pedicures are up to you and perhaps your husband. I know one husband who likes his wife to paint her toenails but hates fingernails polished.

Teeth are important. Not just keeping them clean. Keeping them! This means a dentist with an eye on them at least twice a year. And it means having work done the minute it should be. Don't go around with a chipped tooth.

A well-controlled body is much more beautiful than a body with artificial support pushing it around. I feel very strongly about the gentle and natural lines that are so often distorted. Diet and exercising are better than tight lacing. American women have a kind of easy-going slouched posture that I don't object to if a reasonable amount of slenderness is present. I think that the sternly girdled never look as happy or as relaxed or as graceful as those who wear light underpinnings. I think the mass production of the uplift brassiere has distorted so many American bodies it should be ashamed of itself. All emphasis has been concentrated in one place. I am willing to predict that this will be the laughed-at style twenty years from now, as the exposed legs of the '20s are laughed at today. Today, the "bowed" Charleston girls look just plain funny—the too-pointed overemphasized '50s will, too. Venus didn't wear one.

Some of you may misread this chapter, go away thinking you don't have to do anything about your figure. If you will reread, you will find that I am applying the same principles to beauty that I have applied to Fashion. Never too much, never too little, never undue exaggeration, never downright carelessness. Ask yourself first of all: "Have I done my best to keep myself trim, without the danger of starvation diets, overexercise? Am I weight-conscious? Do I ever walk?" Now if there are certain serious disproportions after you have done your part, you will obviously need the support of firmer underthings. But this does not mean punishing, rigid, unrelenting foundations.

I believe in going to the experts when weight is a problem. A doctor who understands you and your diet. Don't enroll in a gymnasium and do workouts that would tire an Olympic champion. Go to a recognized beauty salon and learn a few A-B-C exercises that will reduce you where you need reducing. And don't be a bore about it all. Don't drive your husband and your friends crazy by talking about your diet all the time.

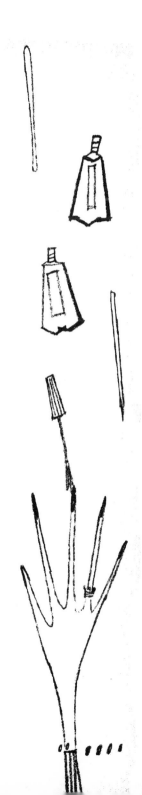

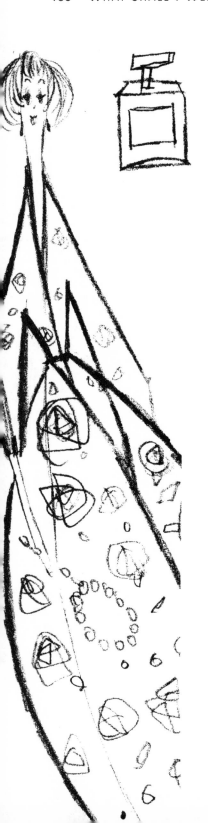

Give good health all the credit it deserves in any beauty program. You don't need to have unshiny hair, brittle nails, a troubled complexion. If you need dress shields, make a separate contraption out of elastic and shields. They fit you, not the dress, and can be worn with any type armhole.

Beauty is concerned with the same kind of thing Fashion likes. Color—in your lipstick as well as in your sash. Shape, in eyebrows and figures and hairline, to harmonize with hatline and silhouette. Pretty toes to dress up open-toe shoes.

Enjoy the fun of it all. Collect bottles and boxes and jars like jewelry for a pretty dressing table. But collect discriminately.

Beauty, like Fashion, is sometimes silly on purpose. Think of a twenty-year-old deliberately adding a streak of gray to her hair! Only she thinks of it as Fashion and there is nothing wrong with it if it makes her feel glamorous and if it's done by an expert. Artificial eyelashes looking artificial on purpose are wonderful if you want to play with them. Even Victorian ladies whimsically stuck on beauty spots. Beauty and Fashion go together, need each other, and you and I need them both.

CHAPTER 14

"DEAR MISS McCARDELL ... MY DAUGHTER INSISTS ON WEARING ...

DRESSING YOUR FAMILY takes tact, imagination, some du-
plicity (they must never know you are doing it), and a
knowledge of what to look for in answer to their specific
needs and tastes.

The chapter heading is a quote from a distraught mother
coping with a current teen-age "sin"—wearing sheer nylon
blouses with blue jeans. The mother was approaching the
problem from the point of: "How can she still be modest and
keep up with this awful teen-age fashion?" She asked me quite
simply to *please* design some underwear that would look nice
under all that transparency.

To me, the sensible thing would be to get rid of the nylon
blouse, but the mother probably knew that it was hopeless
at this particular point to get her daughter *out* of that nylon
blouse. She was apparently coping with an emergency. And
I am inclined to agree that sometimes it may be wiser to try
to mend matters rather than to forbid. Especially when you've
come head-on into the very special world of teen-agers. You
can only hope that the fad will die out quickly. You *might* be
able to hurry its demise by thinking up something *really* trend-
setting to wear with blue jeans. But the latter proposes a
daughter who has something of the trend-setter in her, and
that doesn't always happen.

I think, if I were a mother in a situation like this, I would
try *both* methods. I would make quite sure that *when* and *while*
my daughter insisted on the sheer nylon blouse, she looked

attractively clad beneath it. Back to the old-fashioned camisole if necessary, with its sturdy cotton bodice and eyelet embroidery. But at the same time I would be literally wracking my brain to think of some *new* kind of top for blue jeans, something that would be a far better mate than sheer nylon and that would intrigue a teen-age audience. Once of the very best big-timers was the pink shirt, man-tailored, but very feminine and appealing with collar open and sleeves casually rolled. It was introduced by a fashion magazine and re-introduced by a nationwide picture magazine, and every woman, from teens to thirties and on up lovingly adopted it.

I might add at this point that teen-age clothes fads are anything *but* a budding Fashion sense. They are all tied up with bebop and bunny hopping and this year's top tune. But don't be discouraged—*it* can happen any time. By "it" I mean the sudden tiring of a Davy Crockett shirt; the rather shy inquiry about a weskit or "a dress that *doesn't* button down the front" as one ten-year-old put it. What a wonderful moment to know that this particular ten-year-old has discovered that not *all* dresses button down the front.

Suddenly, without a word of warning, your very youngest may discover her woman's rights to be fashionable. She may be five, or only four, but she has fixed you with a look that might as well be twenty. She wants something "new" to wear, and furthermore she wants to choose it herself, and the only heartening thing about it is that she isn't particular about how little it will cost. She is not, thank goodness, price-tag-conscious—*yet*. If you are a smart mother you will indulge this whim at once, take her on a shopping tour, steel yourself for hours of indecision, be prepared to do a wonderful job of unobvious steering at necessary moments. This may be the actual moment of the birth of a Fashion sense.

The first shopping trip to a "real store" can be momentous. Don't ever spoil it by an irritable "Don't be silly," or a dogmatic "No, you can't have it, it's too old for you." A certain amount of steering, of course. The angora sweater may come off on her partner's navy-blue suit at her first school

dance. Mine did, and I've never forgotten it. But unless something is in really bad taste, be a little lenient. Even let her have something a little too old if her heart is set on it. "I think I need a kind of thin brassiere"—you can buy it for her for seventy-five cents and she'll undoubtedly keep it in her bureau drawer to look at. Try to give her some idea of what is too obvious, teach her about monotones—a cocoa brown, a soft beige. If you can afford to let her grow up with an appreciation of "special" clothes, buy her a sweater with a label that says "Made in France" and explain what that label stands for. Teach her to look for "nice" buttons—tiny ones with a subdued pearl look. Be sure she looks to see if there is enough hem "to grow in."

Your son, of course, wouldn't be caught dead in a shop with you, but he may surprise you. Suddenly he is going to something that is a little different from the average school dance. It probably isn't going to be a tuxedo problem right now, but it is going to be a dark suit and the "right" tie and a new pair of black shoes. Treat it all as casually as you can, but introduce a good deal of reassurance along the way. The black shoes may strike him as pretty silly. "I bet Bill won't have any." You'll have to do as beautiful middle-path job so that he won't be snobbish about the boys who turn up in brown shoes, but will, at the same time, enjoy the secure feeling of his own "right shoes at the right time and the right place."

An unobtrusive suggestion, the slight steering I've talked about, can make your family aware of well-dressed traditions and rules, can also add to the pleasure of social occasions. You don't want your debutante daughter to look *too* dressed up. Showing her pictures of beautifully dressed women, in the news, in fashion magazines, can do far more than saying "No" to the too-sophisticated dress she is eyeing for her coming-out party.

The older generation needs you, too. Your mother has decided that "over sixty" means black, navy blue, possibly gray. Find her an easy-cut soft tweed suit in a lavender mixture, in a soft blue, a gentle beige—it will soon be her favorite outfit. Remind her that white is her most flattering summer or winter-resort color.

I have just had the fun of designing my first baby clothes collection. I had begun to observe that *all* babies seemed to live in diapers or nighties or old-fashioned kimonos. I didn't blame the young mothers. Nobody would if they could see what baby clothes usually are. Tight little sleeves hard to pull chubby little arms into, choking necklines, too many buttons to button (and maybe get swallowed). I tried to apply my easy to live in, easy to get into, easy to keep in shape princi-ples. Things tied to fit. All-in-one sleeves with easy shoulder room—made to open for easy ironing. Stripes and polka dots on "Baby McCardells" are just as much fun as smocking and rosebuds and why shouldn't a baby boy start with tab collars! Of course it was all wonderful fun for me. I went on to tiny saddle shoes and miniature Mary Janes and V-necklines in-stead of the eternally round neck or Peter Pan collar. I was thinking of comfort first, for the baby and for the mother, and I couldn't help thinking how lazy we all are about accepting what's been going on forever. You can start something-new-to-wear for *your* child just as well as I can. Of course you know how to sew ....

Every woman should at least be able to sew on a but-ton—otherwise she's hardly a woman. After that, she mends things: her husband's socks, those shirt buttons, name tapes for the children off to school or camp, her own lingerie straps. Not much perhaps but still *sewing*. These are the dull angles.

There are things to be done with clothes you buy that will make them yours. Things to do with your daughter's "store dress" that will make it hers. Take a cashmere sweater, expensive, but the buttons are the same as those you'd find on any old three dollar sweater. Change them. Buy some little charm-type buttons—softer, more interesting than all the dec-orated sweaters in the world. Put two kinds of buttons on one sweater: it makes it a real sweater of your own. Choose but-tons that will blend with your jewelry or your sports clothes.

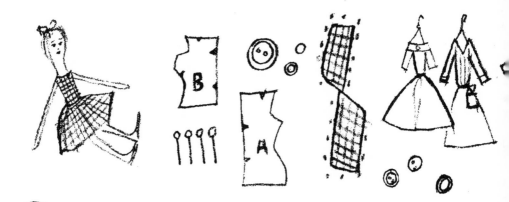

If you can sew, not as a professional—I don't mean that—
you can change your old clothes and keep them in fashion.
Sometimes bringing an old dress up to date is far better than
buying something new that you aren't sure of—that you will
have to get used to. It's a challenge, of course. To remake or
do a simple remodeling job may sound impossible. Actually,
it's often quite easy. A matter of hemline, a change in neckline
or shoulderline. Sleeves shortened or removed entirely. All
these fundamentals in a dress can be changed if you can sew.
And if you love something—patch it, keep it!

Any woman who *can't* sew is a question mark for a
prospective husband. No one is perfect; no one is born with
all talents and all aptitudes; but we *can* learn, have the ability
to develop new skills, whether we're sewing or cooking or
telling Junior what to do next. Fashion makes the same demands of flexibility. You must grow with Fashion, just as
you grow with Junior, otherwise you may meet a college
friend on the street and discover you are living in the wrong
century.

Knowing how to remodel your own clothes, your children's clothes, is one of the best ways to keep up with Fashion. And with the head start of a dress already put together,
you may feel far more confident about plunging into dressmaking via the remodeling route. If you change the appearance of
the dress even slightly, you will feel the first glow of creation.

Of course if you don't know even the basic techniques of sewing, you'll have to learn. My advice is to enroll in a sewing school. All the books on sewing won't do you very much good unless you have seen with your own eyes how each step is taken. You can waste hours trying to decipher a pattern or learn a new stitch from a diagram, but if someone *shows* you the trick the thing will really register. Miss Annie sat on one side of the sewing machine and I sat beside her. We both faced the same way so I could see just what her fingers were doing. This is the principle the Army uses in its training courses. The teacher does not stand up in front; he is directly behind the student, his hands and the hands of the student working in unison.

I never did learn to sew really well, but I got an effect, you might say. I was always in such a hurry to try on my creations that I didn't have the patience to make them carefully. Usually, I made things over—trying everything—coats, suits, hats, fancy-dress costumes. When I first came to New York to study at the Parsons School of Design, I lived at the Three Arts Club and there I had a chance to see my first "Paris" clothes. The ladies of the Board used to sell us their fabulous castoffs for five dollars a dress. I bought all I could afford, managed to make them fit, saw how they were put together and developed my first admiration for the exquisite Parisian way of dressmaking.

When I transferred to the Paris branch of Parsons I soon found out that the Paris *couture* sells its models at a fraction of their original price when the collection showings are over. I went to many sales, tried on, bought, made over. And all the time I was learning important things, the way clothes worked, the way they felt, how they fastened, where they fastened.

Study the workmanship in the clothes in your own wardrobe. If you see something on sale that you could never have been able to afford at its original price, buy it—even if it *is* a little too big. Make up your mind to alter it yourself. If you get into trouble a professional tailor or dressmaker can always rescue you. But if the dress is too small, do a little detecting. Turn the dress inside out. What do the seams tell you? *Where* is it too small? Letting out often involves no more than a half-inch, but is there that half-inch where you need it? And remember, any seam, ripped and resewn, must have at least an eighth of an inch on each side of the stitching to hold without ripping.

Remodeling will get your hand in, reassure you, stimulate you, and suddenly one day you will see an entrancing bolt of fabric and begin to dream it into a dress. And who knows you may graduate some day to a real dress dummy approximating your own measurements.

But at the start, be smart about short-cuts, and patterns so difficult they may defeat you. The easy all-in-one sleeve is simple to fit, universally becoming, and can't be topped for comfort. Intricate set-in sleeves, a dress with dozens of separate pieces to juggle together, may rob you of all the joys of sewing. Learn on a doll's dress! The principles of sewing can be applied in miniature just as well as in your own size. Applied well they work well and with wonderfully satisfying results.

CHAPTER 15

FASHION HAS NO LAST CHAPTER

FASHION IS A continued story—and a continuing one. It is birth and reincarnation, more positive than negative, never really arbitrary. Every rule in the book has been or will be broken—successfully—to start a new Fashion. That's the exhilaration of it all; that's the challenge and the fun. Keep remembering that Fashion is fickle, that it changes constantly, never stands still. Take advantage of its flexibility and make some new rules. Keep investigating that wonderful phrase "Why not?"

There is a great deal in common between the woman who designs cloths and the woman who knows clothes. They both think in very much the same terms. I am often asked by students just what a designer must learn. Look over my list—see how many rules apply to a sound awareness of what good Fashion is. In my speech to prospective designers I refer to:

THE ESSENTIAL ELEVEN

1. Learn to see
2. Learn to sew
3. Learn to drape
4. Learn color
5. Learn anatomy
6. Learn to wear clothes well and appropriately
7. Learn the difference between good taste and bad taste
8. Learn what sells and what doesn't
9. Learn fashion history—trends—cycles
10. Learn how to feel changes before they come
11. Learn how to know when they're gone

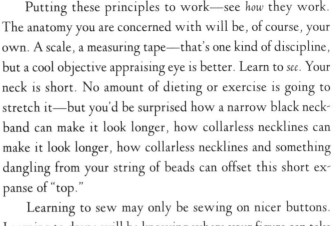

Putting these principles to work—see *how* they work. The anatomy you are concerned with will be, of course, your own. A scale, a measuring tape—that's one kind of discipline, but a cool objective appraising eye is better. Learn to *see*. Your neck is short. No amount of dieting or exercise is going to stretch it—but you'd be surprised how a narrow black neckband can make it look longer, how collarless necklines can make it look longer, how collarless necklines and something dangling from your string of beads can offset this short expanse of "top."

Learning to sew may only be sewing on nicer buttons. Learning to drape will be knowing where your figure can take draping. A fish-tail back is wonderful if you have nothing much jutting above it. A surplice is a strategic disguise for a too-full bosom.

Color is often mood as well as matching: to match or not to match, a decision of "Shall I be understated?" or "Do I want to be striking?" The conventional rules you learned in school about "this goes with that" are seldom related to the fashion palette. Remember, you did it by opposites: red and green, blue and yellow. Fashion is much more apt to say red and yellow; blue and green.

How to wear clothes, when to wear what, is the whole story of dressing appropriately, showing good taste. What sells and what doesn't is just common caution if you're in the designing business. But it's important for you, too. You don't want to make an expensive mistake. You don't want to have bought the one thing nobody would be caught dead wearing. What *not* to buy is often very personal: "My husband hates me in pink." "Where would I wear it?"

Fashion history may not concern you but certainly trends and cycles will. And there is no excuse for "other world" ignorance. Fashion magazines vie with each other to report straws in the wind; are the first to sign off on a tired fashion. You'll know, without second sight or an inner ear, what may very well be going to happen soon. And that, of course, takes care of my last two points. If you really want to look as if you love Fashion, find it morale building, helpful to your career, or just plain gratifying to you yourself—give yourself every chance to be in on the new and off with the old.

I think it is important for you to decide on which designer is designing closest to your own ideas of clothes. Even if your clothes budget is small, there is a fascinating difference in two dresses, each priced at $29.95, with the labels of two different designers or manufacturers identifying them. And the thesis holds true when you move into higher brackets. The names of certain very high-fashion designers will be linked not only with beautiful workmanship, fine fabrics, high price tags—but also with a certain way of life and often a certain age bracket.

Mainbocher does not expect college girls to buy his clothes, but that does not mean that he is in any sense limited as a creator. He deliberately limits himself, as most designers do. We specialize in what we like best, in what we do best, and in what satisfies us most deeply. For me, it is American— what looks and feels like America. It's freedom, it's democracy, it's casualness. it's good health. Clothes can say all that.

Like most designers I used to make two trips a year to Europe to see the Paris collections; to learn from them; to be inspired by them; to be, inevitably influenced by them. But somehow I had a feeling that I wanted to do a different kind of clothes. I began to experiment, just following basic trends instead of copying exactly or frankly imitating here and there—the usual dress-business procedure. I translated my idea into American fabrics, made things I'd seen in Paris a little easier, a little more casual, a little less self-conscious—a little *more* American. The term "American Look" came into the Fashion vocabulary, usually applied to what the trade calls sports clothes—but this is really a fallacy. I've said before in this book that a jersey or a tweed (notably sports clothes fabrics) can go to tea with Aunt Bess. I prefer to think of sports clothes as clothes uninfluenced by Paris—clothes that wield *their own* influence. You have seen how wool jersey can even make evening clothes.

American women are the most beautiful and the best proportioned in all the world. They have fine legs, good feet, healthy color, shining hair. They are not hard to dress. On the other hand, they are not erect and queenly. They have a posture of their own, a comfortable, easy, casual way of moving. Their walk is swinging, not mincing; in tune with all the places they are always off to—a job, the golf links, the market, the club.

I have tried to express all this in my clothes and I think that even the high priests of Fashion are beginning to believe that Fashion can give something individual to American women.

I still go back to Paris, and always shall, to breathe its stimulating air, to see and buy fine fabrics, to admire the work of the very talented fingers that produce out of sheer love of beauty and form. But I always remember that I belong to a mass-production country where any one of us, all of us, deserves the right to good Fashion, and where Fashion must be made available to us all.

I urge you again to buy yourself a present, even if it's a once-in-a-lifetime present, something "made for you"—remembering that you can never quite equal the joy of a dress or a hat or a shoe that is made for you. Maybe in Paris—and that, I promise you, would be more than just a joy. Even in an age of mass production at the highest level, a bit of wearing apparel that is *your* choice, your exact measurements, the kind and color of fabric that you alone decide upon—well, it's a joy forever and what's more you'll probably keep it forever. It won't be like your grandmother's wedding dress, packed away to yellow with age. The hemline will go up and down, the waistline will adjust to this year's trend. And even with changes, it will remain individual, beautiful, yours—and always in fashion.

To go back, in this last chapter, to the principles that govern both the designing and the *knowing* of good clothes, I shall give you the same straight-from-the-mind talk that I give to young people graduating from designing school. To know clothes, either as a designer or as a woman who earns the title "well-dressed," you must first of all love clothes and be willing to train your eye and your mind so that good points register and bad points reveal. This doesn't mean sitting in an ivory tower spinning dresses in silk and satin. It means putting on your down-to-earth glasses and studying; gaining a first-hand knowledge of what you can expect of certain fabrics (you can't expect jersey to billow and taffeta won't ever really cling). Learn to put certain colors together for elegance; certain other colors together for flair.

Acquire dollars and sense knowledge. S-E-N-S-E. A designer's mistake in dollars and sense can cost her employer thousands of dollars. In a way, your $100 or $50 mistake can be just as devastating. Even if your husband grins and bears it, your own sense of guilt will punish you and your wardrobe may suffer a serious defection. The $100 us spent, the dress has been mercifully given away so you don't have to be reminded of it, but perhaps there isn't another $100 available to replace your bad buy and perhaps you will actually have to decline an invitation because you have nothing suitable to wear. (The long dress when long-dress is explicit, is an example.)

Of course you'll make mistakes, I made one just the other day. For some reason I decided to try an elastic band in a cotton jacket. Instead of clinging casually, the jacket curled up and died. But you will learn from your mistakes and you'll never stop trying new things, learning about new things, and I can tell you from experience, you'll never stop learning.

I also tell prospective designers to collect plenty of energy. I tell you who are going to become an expert on clothes to do likewise. You can't let the alarm clock ring and fall into your clothes, expecting to turn up at the office looking fresh and serene and well-dressed.

I add another maxim. "Learn to make decisions and stick to them." I have had to make myself rule out certain kinds of clothes, decide on what's for my line. You will have to rule out certain kinds of clothes that are not for your figure, or your life, or your temperament. And last, perhaps most im-

portant, you must do more than what it takes to just "get by."
The well-dressed woman, like the designer who is earning
her way, knows that the perfect costume is *not* assembled by
osmosis. Osmosis, besides being one of those crossword-puz-
zle words, has a dictionary meaning, a kind of vague meaning.
It is defined as a lucky happenstance, something that occurs
in transit.

Luck may play an occasional role, but not very often. The
perfectly turned-out woman, harmonious in herself, her role,
her surroundings, is the women who has planned it that way.
Nothing whimsical in her choice of beige and black. She
knows it says sophisticated elegance. This year's headlines
have no influence on her choice of straight lines. She knows
that fashion silhouettes have always, *will* always, include the
sheath with its straight lines becoming to her figure, along
with other silhouettes that other figures may like better. No
Christmas present was responsible for those white kid gloves.
She considers them a part of her wardrobe. She doesn't look
as if she's thrown a single dollar away on fluff, and if she has
economized somewhere (as she probably has) it doesn't show.
One taxicab going eight blocks in New York at a crowded
hour can cost *nearly* the price of a pair of stockings and certainly the price of a new lipstick. You'd be surprised how
often this well-dressed, well-groomed woman *walks*. And not
only to have extra change in her purse but to keep her body
in training.

The *only* serious thing about Fashion is this pre-planning,
pre-buying moment. Every smart woman knows that Fashion
is supposed to be fun but that it won't be fun if you don't
know what to expect of it. So give it some serious thought

beforehand. "What do I expect of the Fashion?" Will it answer what I expect of it?" Beforehand planning and thinking and questioning are part and parcel of the Fashion world. Dyes are tested before they are applied to fabrics. Fabrics are tested before a manufacturer dreams of telling you they will take sun or soap and water And in the dressmaking field itself, everything moves in steps; thought about, considered the whole way. The sketcher sketches but the pattern-maker says, "It won't work." The next test is when the dress is modeled—"so it is going to rip under the arms." Fashion reporters are on hand long before your planning begins, their experienced eyes pre-decide for you; they are adept in their judgment that the buyers make notes of the numbers that have been selected to be shown in magazines and newspapers.

You are lucky to have had all this preliminary work done for you. When you see a dress that *fits* your plan, you can be certain that it has been sifted. (That's a curious word but it says what I feel. Designing, like cooking, has to be measured and timed and tested all along the line.) But the last word in Fashion, like the last word in cooking, is yours. Which recipe? What kind of menu? *You* make the decision. What will *you* wear?

"McCARDELLISMS"

A GLOSSARY OF TERMS
THAT SPEAK TO ME
OF FASHION ... AND
HAVEN'T VERY MUCH TO
DO WITH WEBSTER ...

NIGHTGOWN SILHOUETTE: Beloved high waistline, comfortable, easy. demands small rib line, makes all legs look longer. An uncorseted look, a revolution against discomfort in clothes, recurring often as a protest when you can't breathe or move in tight lacings; and it covers a bad hip line with ease.

KITCHEN-DINNER DRESS: For the cook who is the hostess. She cooks in the kitchen; you eat the dinner there—but it's the best cooking you have ever had, and probably the best-dressed cook.

PANTS: Short, long, tight, full; shorts, ski pants, riding pants, jodhpurs, blue jeans.

T-SQUARE: Cut with sleeves like a T-Square, often a beach cover.

ROUGH-DRY: Cotton fabric that dries with a crinkle, no ironing.

HOOKS and EYES: Fastening for belts or fronts of dresses.

SNAPPERS: Jackets, blouses, pants snap on and off.

POCKET: A necessity in every dress, usually useful, but sometimes a line to mark a hip bone—also a place to put your hands.

STORM COAT: Rain, snow, sleet—warm inside, waterproof outside; strapped together, covers everything—suits in town, ski clothes in winter.

SWATCH: The clipping of fabric I carry around to inspire me to make a new dress for you.

COAT: Anything that does over everything else. You can be "coated" in a stole.

POPOVER: Something that goes over anything. It is an apron one day, a bathrobe the next, a dinner dress, if necessary with lots of beads.

MONASTIC: Gunny sack, stringbean, any dress without a waistline, to be belted or sashed as you like it.

DRESS-SHIRT: A dinner shirtwaist dress, easy, comfortable, sit-on-the-floor type; rugged fabric that wears.

STRIP-TEASE or MATCHES: Clothes in pieces. You can wear all of them at one time or only two or three pieces—but they go together and are made of related fabrics.

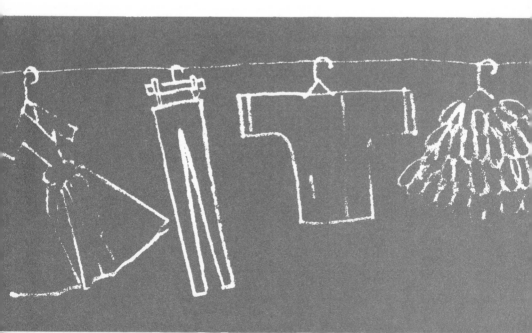

FIGURE: It means, of course, the size you are. It is taken for granted that none of you are overweight; it is accepted as fact that none of you are perfectly proportioned. Not *all* average-figure faults are found, however, in a single female. The ideal is seldom seen outside of fashion drawings: legs inhumanly long, waist incredibly small, enough and not too much of everything else. But you can *learn* from the ideal. Highlight the spots that co-incide — a really small waist, for instance. Soft-pedal the places that are *out* of line — no slim, straight skirts for wide hips is a case in point. When I say "Small" in this book I am thinking of 5 feet; Medium is the range between 5 feet 3 inches and 5 feet 5 inches; Tall is model height, over 5 feet 5 inches. Small waist: at least 12 inches smaller than bust and hip measure.

MODEL: A girl you can't compete with unless Nature gave you a head start and you are willing to starve, exercise, go to bed early, learn a special walk. But you can learn self-discipline from her.

HEMLINES and WAISTLINES: Very definitely Datelines.

GLITTER: Usually to be avoided; never to be added to "shiny."

TYPE: What people tell you you are to flatter you; not always a compliment.

HAT: Anything on your head; it could even be a straw bracelet encircling your topknot.

McCARDELL HEEL: Illusion: elegance. No illusion: its low-slung comfort.

SASH: Anything that ties around your waist, as opposed to belts, which have set fastenings.

FASHION: An indefinable something that every woman would *like to* know.

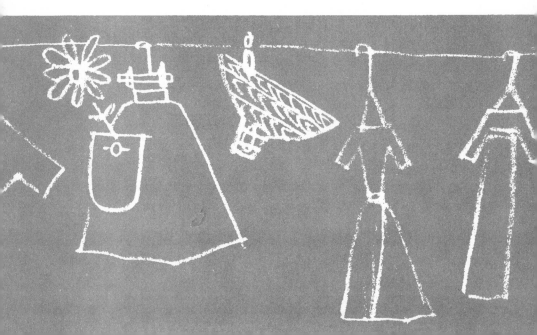